Recurring Dreams
A Journey to Wholeness

By Kathleen Sullivan

To Jean,
May we travel together in dreamland

Kathleen
Sept. 2005

D1115470

❋

THE CROSSING PRESS
FREEDOM, CALIFORNIA

Copyright © 1998 by Kathleen Sullivan
Cover photograph by Lily
Interior design by Leigh McClellan and Victoria May
Printed in the U.S.A.

Grateful acknowledgment is made for permission to reprint excerpts from previously published material:

Chopra, Deepak, *Perfect Weight*, Crown Publishers, New York, NY, © 1994.

Estés, Clarissa Pinkola, Ph.D., *Women Who Run With the Wolves*, Ballantine Books (division of Random House, Inc.), New York, © 1992, 1995.

Leonard, Linda Schierse, *Witness to the Fire: Creativity and the Veil of Addiction*, Shambhala Publications, Inc., Boston, MA, © 1989.

O'Connor, Peter, *Dreams and the Search for Meaning*, Paulist Press, Mahwah, NJ, © 1986.

Sams, Jamie and David Carson, *"Eagle" From Medicine Cards*, Bear & Company Publishing, Santa Fe, NM, © 1988.

Sanford, John A., *Dreams and Healing*, Paulist Press, Mawah, NJ, © 1978.

Sanford, John A., *The Invisible Partners*, Paulist Press, Mahwah, NJ, © 1980.

Wilber, Ken, *Grace and Grit*, Shambhala Publications, Inc., Boston, MA, © 1991.

Wolf, Fred Alan, *The Dreaming Universe*, Simon & Schuster, New York, NY, © 1994 by Wolf Productions.

For information on bulk purchases or group discounts for this and other Crossing Press titles, please contact our Special Sales Manager at 800-777-1048.

Visit our Website on the Internet at: www.crossingpress.com

Library of Congress Cataloging-in-Publication Data
Sullivan, Kathleen, 1941-
     Recurring dreams : a journey to wholeness / by Kathleen Sullivan.
        p. cm.
     Includes bibliographical references.
     ISBN 0-89594-892-3 (pbk.)
     1. Dreams. 2. Dream interpretation 3. Self-actualization (Psychology)—Miscellanea.
I. Title.
BF1091.S814 1998
154.6'3--dc21
                                                      98-5020
                                                       CIP

This book is dedicated to all who have the courage and commitment to honor their dreams. And especially to you who have invited me to hear and work with your dreams, deep gratitude. Because of what you have taught me, I can better understand and share my own work.

Acknowledgements

I am deeply grateful to the following people for their participation in this project. Each has been instrumental in the quality of the finished product. Thanks to Barbara Nelson and Lee Marchitelli for unwavering support from beginning to end; to all the readers and loving critics: Don Wobber, Lisa Barkalow, Harriet Berman, Ann Jacobson, Kelly Bulkeley, Judy Tatelbaum, Sheila Sheppard, Mary Collins-Shields, and Reda Rackley-Smith; to Larry Fobian for emergency technical support at all hours; to Barbara and Guido Marchitelli and Shirley Mattraw for providing beautiful and inspirational writing environments; to Gary Cooke who believed in me through it all; and finally deepest loving thanks to Mary Thiele Fobian, devoted and creative midwife, humorous companion, and editor extraordinaire. And finally, profound gratitude to all of my teachers, living and dead.

Contents

Foreword

One of my favorite stories about dreams comes from the Bible, in the first book of Samuel. When Samuel (who would one day become a great leader of the people of Israel) was still a young boy, he and his father Eli were tending the Temple which housed the Ark of the Covenant, the holiest of holy objects to the Israelites. One night, while Samuel slept inside the Temple, he thought he heard a voice calling him. He awoke, and went outside to Eli, saying, "Here I am!" But Eli said it wasn't him who had called Samuel. So the boy walked back into the Temple and went to sleep. Again he heard the voice calling him, and again he went out to ask Eli what he wanted. But Eli said it wasn't him, so Samuel returned once more to the Temple. When the voice called Samuel a third time, Eli realized that it was not a human voice calling the boy in his sleep, but the voice of God. So when Samuel lay down in the Temple once more and heard the voice speaking to him, he didn't get up, but instead said, "Speak, Lord, for thy servant hears." And finally, with Samuel ready to listen at last, God shared with the boy a wondrous dream revelation, an inspiring vision of what the future would hold for him and his people.

Although this story comes in a religious context, I believe it teaches us something very important about the power of dreams, whether or not we consider ourselves to be religious or spiritual people. The story suggests that to learn from our dreams, we must first pay attention to them—we have to be ready to listen to them and hear what they have to say. Fortunately for us, our dreams can be quite insistent when they have an important message to convey. Just as Samuel's dreams kept coming until Eli helped him recognize how important they were, our own dreams often keep coming, pestering and prodding us until we recognize what they are trying to express.

Recurring Dreams: A Journey to Wholeness tells the story of a latter-day Samuel, a person whose dreams literally seized her life and guided her through a series of difficulties and crises into a future of remarkable discovery, achievement, and fulfillment. Kathleen Sullivan's "dreamography" shares with readers her experiences with the incredibly transformative energies that emerge in our dreams. Kathleen is a born teacher, and her book speaks both to newcomers to the dream world as well as to people who have some experience in exploring that mysterious realm of the imagination.

Although *Recurring Dreams* is written in very gentle, down-to-earth prose, readers should know that it is based on cutting-edge dream research. From the theories of the great pioneer of dream psychology Carl Jung to the latest findings of sleep laboratory research, everyone who studies dreams now recognizes that especially fruitful discoveries can be made by studying dream *series*: the deepest currents of the unconscious can be discerned most clearly across the course of several dreams.

The various dream series that Kathleen describes in this book illustrate better than any research article ever could the life-changing powers of dreaming. Kathleen has truly lived what she writes about, and this makes her book a rare pleasure to read.

—Kelly Bulkeley, Ph.D.
President of the Association for the Study of Dreams
Kensington, California

Preface

An autobiography tells the story of a human life. This dreamography tells about the restoration of a human life through the workings of the dream.

The *human story* is about a professional American woman caught in a web of chronic illness, addiction, and depression. The *dream story* is about an inner process seemingly determined to expose and dissolve the strangulating strands of the web, strung, in part, during a childhood of parental alcoholism, mental illness, and financial precariousness. By submitting to guidance from her dreams each strand has been severed, allowing this woman the freedom and courage to soar.

As you read the dreamography on the following pages, I trust you will see human dreaming as much more than random nightly entertainment or the brain's process of sorting through the events of daily life. Instead, you will recognize the majesty of a deep inner process which has focus, direction, brilliance, humor, and profound intention to dissolve the lethal hold of the webs that could bind any of us.

I hope this book will appeal to novice dream students unfamiliar with their inner process, as well as old pros who delight in seeing the evolution of psyche over time. Time is relative, of course; thirty-five years is insignificant to a redwood tree, but to a human struggling for awareness, it's a fair history.

This dreamography tells of two interlocking series of dreams. The first features psyche's determination to reunite me with "someone" deemed vitally important (the Reunion Series). The second, simultaneous series presents my evolving relationship with that "someone," who provided guidance which eventually leads to major transformation (The Victor Biento Series). The Eagle Dream which begins this book provided the jarring demands that eventually led me to research and write about both of these series.

It is my purpose to do more than tell an interesting and unusual story. I hope to motivate you, the reader, to watch, play with, study, and manifest your own dreams. (To this end I offer basic dream tending suggestions in the Introduction which follows.) I know that when we go beyond the limitations of our conscious selves into the broader, deeper, and higher spiritual domains of the dream, we become more whole, more satisfied, less frightened and controlling, more giving and loving. I've watched and treasured this evolution in myself and hundreds of associates, friends, and clients over the years. I delight in living with ever-increasing numbers of people experiencing this transformation, leading me to this hopeful game of WHAT IF:

WHAT IF we could create a society arising more from conscious choice than from the domination of unrecognized familial and cultural scripts which engender, generation after generation, dysfunctional individuals, families, and cultures?

WHAT IF we nurtured the authentic self which becomes visible, one sparkling facet at a time, as individuals understand and actualize their nightly dream material?

WHAT IF millions of individuals learned to identify and transform their own inner darkness, instead of projecting it onto other individuals, cultural groups, and countries?

WHAT IF our physical health and quality of life could be enhanced by understanding dream messages?

I trust this book will illustrate these and more benefits of dreamwork. As you read, I hope you will be able to imagine how the dream process can heal and guide you.

Author's Disclaimer

Throughout this book I have told the truth as I remember it, as I know it. Personal truth alters as time polishes the clarity of perception. Years from now, as I expand my understanding of human development, of psyche, of the dream, what I have written here may seem inaccurate. And surely those who knew me would likely alter, to some degree, what has been written here. We all look through different lenses, have a different view of the same room and arrive at different interpretations of any scene. These are the inevitable foibles of story telling concretized in written form and every author must accept this to be at peace with her/himself and the process of self-exposure.

I want to be clear about another complication specific to this dreamography. You are reading a selection of dreams from the Victor Biento series but by no means all of the dreams that have flashed upon my inner screen in the dark of night. This book contains less than half of the dreams in this series and only the ones that seemed to create certain categories.

I say this to give a more complete and accurate picture of the dream process. Without this disclaimer you might get the idea that dream work is very tidy, always understandable, and categorically intact. That is definitely not the case. To be comfortable with this mysteriously fascinating inner work we must be willing to live in an open-ended process which creates more questions than answers. That accepted, the rewards are endless.

Introduction

Each chapter in this book addresses a different issue raised by my recurring dreams and connects these issues to different elements of dream interpretation. In each chapter you will find dreams from my journal and move from them through my process of exploration and interpretation. You will come to understand that examining some dreams is a very uncomfortable and confusing experience. I share moments when I resisted my dreams' messages and their challenges as well as times when I easily and happily realized a dream's insights.

Each chapter contains ideas from other knowledgeable dream thinkers addressing aspects of dream interpretation with which I wrangled. Following each chapter are exercises for Inner Exploration encouraging you to apply the ideas to your own dream work. These exercises may be done in any order or all together as a mini-dream course.

To that end you may need some rudimentary dream collecting and tending suggestions. First you must choose the type of recording device that most appeals to you. I find using the computer distances me from the emotions and poetry of the dream. In addition, I frequently illustrate dream images, which greatly enhances my connection to the dream. And finally, I use colored pens to better capture the mood of the dream scenes. This I could not do with my computer.

Buy a journal which appeals to you, or create your own. Record on typewriter or computer if that suits your style. Because of the fleeting nature of dream memory, the material must be recorded immediately upon awakening. A tape recorder works well for this if you have a great deal of material and very little time before you hurry into the day. You can train yourself to wake up during the night and record your material then. You can quickly return to the altered state which invites sleep once more by thinking about the dream after the light goes out.

Title and date your dream material. Short comments about the day or days preceding the dream may help to see if the awake world has triggered the dream. Do not edit your material as you write it, but do make margin notes if some part of the dream is upsetting or embarrassing to you. Refrain from judging or quickly interpreting the dream. After it has been safely captured and recorded, ponder, wonder, associate, write about, and share with others who honor the dream. After the dream stews and brews for awhile, return to your journal and write some more.

Be willing to challenge the beliefs, attitudes, and behaviors of dream ego, the "you" in the dream. Honor all the dream elements, not just your bias about one part or perspective of the dream. There are also hundreds of fine dream books available which include extensive suggestions for remembering, recording, and working with your own material.

The most important single element for engaging with your dreams is anticipation. Be excited to embrace the wonder and mystery of this inner art form. Marvel at the part of you that creates such seemingly bizarre, bounteous, intriguing images. Be patient and persistent. After all, you are learning a new language. And it is the language *of* and *from* yourself. Be grateful for every dream you snatch from the demands of the awake world and play with it without requiring cerebral comprehension. Bless every Ah ha! that you experience. In time you will develop a rapport with your dreaming self which can be as important to you as your most intimate relationships.

CHAPTER ONE

Psyche Screams

"Animal dreams provoke their (people's) feelings, get them thinking, interested, and curious. As we get more into imagining, we become more animal like. Not bestial, but more instinctively alive, with more savvy, a keener nose and a sharper ear."

James Hillman, *Dream Animals*

Caught in the Web:
The Eagle Dream   MAY 9, 1980

I'm on a field trip with my class. The kids ahead of me be-
come very excited about something they see which is not yet
visible to me. I run, responding to their pleas, "Hurry, Ms.
Sully! See what we've found!"

When I join them I see an enormous spider's web at least
eighteen feet in diameter. At first I think it is a gorgeous
sight, an awesome display of nature. But then I notice the
Eagle. She is inexorably caught, splayed wing-to-wing, with
her regal head stretched to the left, totally entangled in this
spectacular web.

Suddenly I experience a grief so deep, so devastating, so
all-consuming that I lose all strength in my body. Falling to
my knees, I sob from a place never before accessed. I am over-
whelmed by remorse, by despair.

I awake, carrying the hysteria from the dream into the shattered silence of my bedroom. My pendulum clock sounds the hour of 3:00 A.M. I'm deeply shocked by this experience which feels much more potent than a dream. I struggle to recognize the devastating feelings coursing through my body. For years the sounds of my own cries have awakened me from nightmares but, awake or asleep, I've never felt anything like this. I'm terrified of this unfamiliar out-of-control feeling. I tell myself to snap out of it: "It's only a dream, for heaven's sake. Get a grip!" As if in response my wailing increases, further confounding the part of me that is desperately trying to make sense of this experience.

Finally physical exhaustion returns silence to my usually peaceful home. By 5:00 A.M. the anguish in my heart feels like a lump of frozen ice. I think if

I were pinned under the rubble of an earthquake or had just witnessed a murder I would be able to cope more effectively than this. What the hell has happened here? What does this mean? Can I get out of this lifeless, frigid place to teach school in a few hours? Do I even want to try?

Eventually, habituated behavior kicks in. I get up at the usual time and soak in a hot tub to thaw my frozen feelings and relieve my swollen face. As if a programmed robot, I dress, drink tea, feed the cats, lock the door, and drive to work.

I walk into the staff room hiding my inner darkness and swollen eyes behind sunglasses. I pretend that nothing unusual has happened since I last saw my associates and students. The mundane act of pouring hot water for tea reassures me. I chat casually with a friend, believing I can hide from last night's confounding experience until it slips from memory.

In the classroom, I pretend to be the same teacher I was yesterday, capable of helping a small group of reading students grapple with silent consonants. WHAM! The Eagle flashes behind my eyes. Choking back tears, I flee from the room, leaving an aide in charge.

I hide in the women's lounge, feeling shameful, weak, and stupid. Convinced I am going crazy, I am afraid to approach friends and admit to this dream happening. Denying my trembling, dizziness, and nausea, I tell myself that everything will return to normal within the hour, allowing me to enjoy my weekend as planned.

Clearly, psyche had other plans. How grateful I am today for the power of that single image because it pulled me, kicking and screaming, past the resistance of my intellect and the defenses of my personality. I soon realized that I had to resolve the horror of the Eagle image which had slammed into me with wordless force. Three days after the dream, continuing despair forced me to a therapist. This loving and talented teacher was not well trained in dream-work so he suggested that I replay the dream, hoping that another ending might be envisioned, thus relieving the intense pain that enshrouded me.

After a minor relaxation procedure I recalled the dream and once again relived the physical and emotional trauma I had felt within the dream. As I focused on the agony of the Eagle, she transformed into a tricolored collie dog, jumped out of the web and ran toward me, wagging her tail. "NO!" I screamed. "NO! Get back in the web until you can get out on your own power!" Immediately, the image shifted back to the entrapped Eagle in the web. She suddenly exuded a sense of powerful determination. She no longer seemed pitiful.

I was as flabbergasted by this experience as I was convinced of its validity. Feelings of absolute rightness and acceptance replaced grief and remorse. As I sat quietly watching my therapist watch me, I was aware that I had made a profound decision. I knew that I would devote my life to the extrication of that Eagle. I had no idea what that meant in practical terms, but I was completely committed to whatever the process might be. I also knew that nothing in my life would remain untouched by this decision.

And so, I had heard psyche scream and had taken the first step toward breaking the strands of the web that threatened my very being. Though I didn't know what road lay ahead, nor even the nature of the next step, I did know that *maintaining the integrity of the Eagle* was more important than escaping through the *adaptation of the dog*. A sense of courage and support enveloped me as I relaxed for the first time since the dream. Years later I would read this explanation from James Hillman in *The Soul's Code:* "We often feel what we must do. The image in the heart can lay down strong demands and it asks us to keep faith."

As I left the therapist's office, calmness replaced panic, balance relieved the severe loss of equilibrium. For the first time in my life, I was able to simultaneously access two diametrically opposite types of knowing. I had no doubt about the decision I had made. And I recognized that the part of me that based decisions on rational thinking could make no sense of this at any level. This statement from Anthony Stevens' *Private Myths* explains my process: "The unconscious proposes; the ego disposes. To take on a symbol is to take on the intention of the Self, to cross a bridge from the known to the unknown."

I walked home along the Pacific Grove ocean path, watching seagulls swoop into the surf. Reviewing my feelings since the Eagle Dream, I realized I felt like Alice as she tumbled down the hole. Later I learned to deeply appreciate that analogy; but then, on a warm day in May, I had no cognitive awareness of my descent into the unconscious.

Indeed, at that time I had minimal awareness of my awake-life experience. My denial of my physical and emotional condition was so thick, so dense, that it could be penetrated only when asleep, when my usual guards slumbered. If a friend had approached me with a list of valid concerns about my state of being at the time of the Eagle Dream, I would have responded with a sarcastic wit, rationalizing what was obvious to others but which I minimized. My friend could have pointed to a myriad of physical symptoms which plagued me. I suffered from unceasing headaches, severe loss of energy, and bouts of dizziness that forced me to the floor several times a week and kept me unbalanced at all other times. If my friend reminded me that a variety of medical examinations had been unable to diagnose these indications of severe malaise for almost five years, I would have screamed about the inadequacy of the medical establishment without really admitting to the breadth of my physical problems.

Continuing from the list, my friend could have mentioned the violent mood swings and uncontrollable rages that seemed to spring from a deep, dark, bitter place within me. Reminded of my outbursts in both professional meetings and intimate gatherings—which exposed the feelings of a helpless victim always braced against attack—I would have justified my responses as necessary, right, and laudable.

But perhaps, if my friend had caught me in the vulnerable state after one of my frequent nightmares in the early morning hours, I might have admitted to feelings of despair. I might have voiced fears that I was swimming in a dangerous gene pool which would destroy me prematurely as it had both of my parents, before midlife. I might have acknowledged my well-hidden feelings of terror about the obvious crumbling of my longtime, deeply cherished love relationship. But even hidden by the darkness of predawn, I would have countered my admissions by shrugging my shoulders and telling a funny story to distract my friend. My walls were so thick that no human intervention could have forced me to acknowledge my desperation. Only the image of the dying Eagle was powerful enough to accomplish that.

My need to make sense of the Eagle Dream took over my life. I felt as if an alien had invaded my house during the dark of night, removed my head very painfully from my shoulders, screwed it on backwards, and told me to carry on. The impact of those three days—the never-before-experienced emotional power, the amazing unfolding of the active imagination with my therapist, and my astonishing, peaceful determination—demanded intellectual integration. I had no idea at that time that I would devote the rest of my life to understanding and teaching about that remarkable, alien force, the dream.

My determination to understand the Eagle experience repeatedly led me to Esalen Institute on the Big Sur coast. This center for human development offers some of the world's most renowned teachers in all fields. Each teacher added a useful perspective and dimension to my understanding. I was heartened to discover that everyone with whom I worked valued the dream and the significance of the Eagle experience.

One morning during breakfast at Esalen a pleasant looking man sat near me. As we chatted I told him my dream of that morning. His enthusiastic response led me to tell him the Eagle Dream. This was always a risk for I usually cried during the telling, sometimes causing my confidantes some discomfort. However, this gentleman was so deeply moved that tears came to his eyes. He encouraged me to continue on the path that the dream was leading me. Hugging me warmly, he left with a final admonition to follow the dream, for it would surely guide me well.

At dinner that night someone pointed to my breakfast companion, identifying him as Joseph Campbell, a teacher who would eventually have great impact on my life, but who, on that foggy day in Big Sur, was totally unknown to me.

Each of my teachers provided a different map for my inner journey. Each route I followed allowed me to become more comfortable with my inner process. As I wandered through the dense wilderness of my internal world, my memory retrieved a dream series that had been attempting to guide me for twenty years before the Eagle Dream. Had I known then the power of dreams to identify the direction we need to go and supply guidance along the route; had I been able to comprehend these dreams and the type of energy they wished me to contact; had I been able to participate consciously in the dreams as they unfolded, I strongly suspect the eagle would not have become ensnared.

INNER EXPLORATION

This Inner Exploration section following each chapter encourages you to jump from my pool of consciousness into your own inner work. The questions and exercises can provide structure and focus for contemplation, discussion, or journal-writing. If tending to these exercises within the context of the dreamography disturbs the flow of the story for you, put them aside until later.

Despite the demands of our frantic culture we must create and devote time to value our internal processes. Without this commitment we simply repeat a robot-like existence wherein every tomorrow looks just like every yesterday. By tending to our inner needs we become conscious creators of life rather than its passive victims.

The Call

- Have you ever heard psyche scream? Has a dream or vision threatened your sense of safety and homeostasis? When and how?

- Perhaps you once had such a dream but were unable to deal with it. Are you willing to consider it now, as you continue to read *Recurring Dreams: A Journey to Wholeness*? If so, keep the dream in your awareness and observe your feelings about it.

- Have you watched someone deal with such a dream experience? What about that person's process did you admire or regret?

- If such a dream experience has not grabbed you yet, can you imagine how you would respond? Is this ideally how you would like to react to an inner demand?

- If you should experience a demanding outcry for change, think about all the resources available to you. A little forethought might prepare you to respond with a minimum of resistance if your ego is challenged with a dream as demanding as the Eagle Dream.

- Besides coming through in a dream, in what other ways might you hear psyche scream?

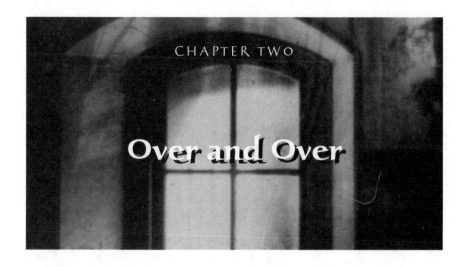

CHAPTER TWO

Over and Over

All of us have emotional residues from our past that we haven't quite disposed of, particular areas of vulnerability that get bruised from time to time in the course of our lives. When this happens, we often have a dream which depicts the problem and shows where we are in relation to it. If we fail to make progress in the particular area that is giving us trouble, we are apt to encounter the same problem again in our lives and to dream about it in the same way.

Montigue Ullman and Nancy Zimmerman,
Working with Dreams

...dreamwork is more than analyzing, explaining, or interpreting dream symbols. It calls for us to stay with the symbol, working and interacting with it, until we are able to release, use, and develop the energy it contains in practical ways.

Louis M. Savary, "Dreamtime"
ASD Journal (Spring 1996)

My motivation to understand the Eagle Dream caused me to search for teachers in various fields of human experience. I followed many paths which eventually led me back to my own process and the nightly messages from my internal teacher, my dreams. There I began to identify and be intrigued by repeating symbols and patterns embedded in my dreams. Eventually I connected to the repeating symbol which is the foundation for this book. Before focusing on the specificity of that symbol, it's important to understand the dynamic of repetitive dreams in general.

Grasping repetitious dream images feels like trying to capture fog as it moves through a dense forest: no image holds steady long enough to make an imprint on my mind's canvas. But finally, repetitive wisps begin to etch themselves into a pattern. I awaken from a dream with a feeling of familiarity. Even within a dream I begin to remember that I've been here before, felt this over and over, or seen that same symbol many times.

Most dreamers are fascinated by repetitive dreams and the questions they stimulate. Why do we have them? What do they mean? Why would one particular dream symbol continuously reappear for many years, on important anniversaries or at crisis points in our lives? What are we telling ourselves, over and over? What is the intent of this persistent dreaming self?

A variety of dream elements may repeat: a theme, a symbol, a character, an emotion or even a vague sensing. In whatever form, repetitive dreams clearly get our attention. Just as we need to repeat any experience—in relationships, at work, or in any aspect of our lives—in order to become aware of the existing dynamic or forming pattern, it seems that dream images need to repeat before we can perceive our psyches' focus and intent.

To illustrate the movement of this repeating energy, here is a series which occurred many years after my parents' deaths.

Caring for the Plants Series
(1983–1987)

This dream series began three years after the Eagle Dream. Driven by my intent to extricate the Eagle, I worked with a therapist to identify the various strands that imprisoned this powerful force. Almost immediately I recognized my need to rescue others and become imprisoned by their problems rather than (and perhaps in order to avoid) focusing on my own. This destructive pattern had begun in early childhood and continued to pressure me throughout adulthood until my therapeutic work began to produce relief.

This inner dynamic was brilliantly portrayed by a dream series that played during a period of nearly four years. Approximately thirty of my dreams presented the repetitive symbol of *plants needing care*. The dream environment, different in every dream, always was identified as my parents' home. At first, the dream's settings were dimly lit shacks. Over the years the shacks evolved into cottages, apartments, and eventually one lovely condo. The final dream of this series takes place in a stunning top-floor apartment.

In nearly every dream, dream ego (the "me" in the dream) became anxious as soon as I realized that I was in my parents' house. Then I felt extreme distress about and responsibility for the care of the many potted plants in my parents' living environment. I knew I must face the plants' condition and that it was my frustrating job to care for these neglected living things.

In most of the dreams, dozens of plants hung from the ceilings, sat on counters, or were supported by free-standing planters. In the beginning, all of the plants were desperately needy, often confined in dark, dingy rooms. Most were dehydrated and near death. The hanging plants had leaves or fronds that had been dead for many years but never trimmed. Some plants sat in smelly, stagnant water, in obvious danger of death from drowning. Others had only two or three healthy leaves.

For the first three years of the series a frantic person—sometimes a girl, sometimes a woman—charged around, trying to rescue and revive these pathetic dying things. Sometimes she cried in frustration, exhaustion, or worry. Occasionally, fury showed on her face as she judged her parents' neglect of these living, growing things. At times the woman sat in despair, apparently feeling it was too late, all was lost.

Toward the end of the third year of this series the images began to change. Many plants were trimmed and tidy. Though some were still over-watered and others thirsty, many looked vibrant in rooms well lit by clean windows. The woman tending the plants appeared more calm, less concerned as she moved from plant to plant, doing what she could.

During the last year enormous changes were obvious. A wide variety of healthy plants were well pruned and tended. The parents often were doing the work, sometimes helped by other people as well. The original caretaking woman was clearly relaxed, even serene as she observed the bountiful, lush beauty that had been nurtured by her and others.

In this series' last dream, dream ego realized she was going to visit her parents' house. The automatic feeling of dread was quickly replaced by cautious anticipation as she recalled that her parents had *hired a full-time gardener.* As she entered the luxurious *upper-level* apartment in which her parents now lived, she saw a bounty of beautiful plants, some exotic and some commonplace, all sizes and types, enhancing every room. In the kitchen, dream ego met the gardener who said, "There is a huge compost pile in the corner by the stove." Clearly everything was now being processed and cared for without the woman's intervention.

To understand the significance of this Plant Series a short family history is necessary. My dreams about being the desperate caretaker accurately express the panic I felt when I was an adolescent responsible for my severely ill mother. Mother's precarious physical and emotional problems began ten years before my birth. To deal with a sudden weight gain, so the story goes, she fasted while drinking only soft drinks and smoking cigarettes. After several weeks of this weight-loss regime, she suffered her first "nervous breakdown" at the age of twenty-five.

During all the years I knew her, Mother rarely ate a normal meal, fearing that she would become fat. She drank at least one six-pack of 12-ounce soft drinks every day and smoked continuously until she died. For the many years that my father managed a bar, she added gin to the Pepsi by early afternoon. In the beginning mother's alcoholism, which relieved her nervousness and depression, was a blessing to me. Violent rages soon replaced that short-lived serenity, including many incidents of throwing cast iron skillets and other objects at my father.

In her early forties Mother's spine began disintegrating, resulting in a series of unsuccessful major surgeries. With the onset of her back problems Mother's chronic "nervous condition" moved into severe clinical depression. For three months she experienced extended catatonic periods which were not alleviated by electric shock treatments. Mother's alcohol addiction was superseded by sleeping pills and morphine after her first surgery.

Except for the times that she was hospitalized, I was the primary caretaker for this desperately unhappy woman in constant physical and emotional agony. I soon began to live in terror of what I might find when I entered the house after an absence. Three times I opened the door to the throat-clenching odor of blood and the sight of Mother's unconscious body and large areas of her bedroom or bathroom stained red. In two of these cases, Mother had sustained head and body gashes from drug-induced falls; in the third episode she slit her wrist, using small sewing scissors. In all three cases, doctors arrived in time to bring her back to a life she clearly felt was not worth living.

After eighteen months of severe mental problems, Mother somehow found her way back to the mind she had lost. However, her connection to it remained tenuous. Three years later, after a total of three ineffective back surgeries, she successfully planned her death and died of an overdose of pills. I was nineteen years old.

In light of this history I hope you can see the obvious metaphors in the Plant Series. Despite my inability to repair her back or to keep Mother from abusing her body through addiction, I was compelled to clean up the messes her illnesses created. I was expected to keep the "dying plants" alive and vital. During Mother's disintegration I had no choice but to assume the futile role of frustrated heroine in a tragic melodrama. I could clean up the blood, but I couldn't stop the falls. As seen in the dream series language, I could water the plants, provide new soil, prune, and feed, but I couldn't control the forces that were perpetually destroying the plants.

I felt a strong need to do more than keep my mother alive physically. I decided I was also responsible for making her happy, for giving her reasons to live. Providing stimulation for a catatonic is as impossible as forcing a drunk to put down the bottle. The desperate needs I felt as an adolescent created a lethal pattern of trying to fix the unfixable. As a youngster I couldn't know the futility of my attempts. As an adult suffering from my own illnesses, my very survival depended upon recognizing this pattern.

What is the meaning of the healthy movement we see in this four-year dream series? Clearly the plants are being effectively tended as the years go by. Since both of my parents were dead at the time of the series, the dreams are speaking of progress within *me* and the ways *I* was healing the patterns from childhood. The Plant Series represents a shift in my behavior with others. This learning continues to this day. Gratefully, I have never suffered a relapse severe enough to reactivate the Plant Series.

A dream series of this magnitude has many levels of meaning. Beyond my reactions to others I was learning to "parent" and nurture myself (the plants) in ways that neither of my parents had been able to model for me. This was happening at the physical level (the proper watering, trimming, transplanting) and the spiritual/mental level (movement from dark, cruddy shacks to the sunny top-floor environment). Breaking the strands of poor self-nurturing and compulsive caretaking were elemental to the eventual release of the Eagle.

If a four-year dream series illustrates significant growth and development, then what intentions could be represented by one particular dream character who appears in my dreams for more than thirty-five years? The next chapter addresses that question and introduces you to the single most valuable and tenacious dream character in my life thus far.

INNER EXPLORATION
Repeating Symbols

- Are you aware of repetitive dream images? Identify what's repeating: an inanimate object, an environment, a smell or a sound, an emotion, a person or animal, or a period of time.

- In your dream journal write a statement of intent concerning your desire to retrieve this dream element from the fog and bring it into the foreground. Begin a system of flagging these images as they repeat.

- When you have a collection of symbols, look at all the data together. See whether and how the repetitious symbols are changing. What do these changes suggest to you?

- What repeating patterns are you aware of in your waking life? What do these patterns suggest to you?

- Is one particular dream character repeatedly making an appearance in your dreams? Pretend that this character has something to give to you. What might that be? Memories? Attributes? Feelings about yourself or a way of being? In your journal write what comes to mind. In the future be on the lookout for this character. Notice whether and how this character changes.

CHAPTER THREE

The Beginning
Reunions

Dreams containing imagery similar to that of previous dreams and associated with similar feelings may occur sporadically or frequently. Such dreams deal with some recurrent issue in the life of a dreamer that has not been set to rest. Although the dreamer borrows images he has used in the past he arranges them in ways that reflect where he is now and what changes, if any, have occurred. Once the issue is resolved, either in reality or through the successful working out of the dream, the repetitive dream ceases.

Ullman and Zimmerman,
Working with Dreams

This story would be easier to tell if consciousness unfolded chronologically. Were that the case, the Eagle experience would begin this dreamography. But it definitely did not. I now know that my psyche had been gently telling me of a desperate need to reunite with a lost part of myself for nearly twenty years before the Eagle shocked me into consciousness. Until the Eagle Dream connected me with the importance of the dream series, I was unable to heed the guidance I was so consistently provided.

To see the brilliance of this persistent inner guidance, we must wind the years back to the early 1960s, for that is when the Reunion Series began. I was twenty years old.

Like most stages of developing consciousness, this series begins with vagueness and lack of recognition. My first conversation about these dreams occurred only because high school friends visited me in San Francisco. What's more natural than casually sharing a bizarre dream with the very people who are imaged in the dream? And so I laughingly reported that I was already having upsetting dreams about our high school reunion, though we had graduated only three years before. "I feel like the dreams are almost nightmares," I said. "I'm very upset and don't want to attend the reunion because I have nothing suitable to wear. On the other hand, for some reason I feel that I *must* go. I awake feeling bitchy and yearning for doughnuts!" After a hearty laugh, the conversation drifted to wild imaginings about what we all would be like at our twentieth reunion.

Throughout the reunion dreams in the 1960s I always sensed a need to attend the get-together in order to see someone who would be there. This desire became a need and finally a painful yearning. I was increasingly frustrated about missing this person, and often would go just to the doorway of the reunion location hoping to see the desired one. Despite the intensity of my longing to see this person, he was never identified in these dreams. All I knew then was that I must reconnect with some man at the reunions.

By the 1970s, the dreams changed, depicting other characters who encouraged me to attend and tried to help me find clothing I could accept. Eventually, I would indeed go to the reunion dance to search for *the* person I so wanted to see. If troubled by my outfit I would overcome my fears of looking foolish and attend anyway. Each experience at the gathering was frustrating because the person I wanted to see was not there.

By the late 1970s the intensity of the search theme became painful. Curiosity and desire were replaced by desperation. Dream ego (the *me* in the dream) felt that she *had to* find this certain person, still unnamed. I remember a conversation in 1978 with my best friend from high school. We tried to imagine who this elusive character was. It was a jovial, goofy session but unproductive in naming the mystery man.

Finally, in 1984, totally unconcerned about clothing, dream ego attends a reunion and sees the one for whom she has been searching for more than twenty years. She sees the person from the back, but recognizes him immediately as a person named *Victor Biento*. (All names of dream characters in this book are pseudonyms.) Though no actual contact is made with him in this dream, dream ego is electrified by the realization that her painful search is finally over. Several years passed before I had a dream in which I actually connected with Victor Biento. And even more time passed before I recognized this particular dream connection and honored it in the awake world.

The reunion series has changed dramatically over thirty years, from my reluctance to go to the reunion to helping others plan the reunion. The clothing problem ended with a delightful dream of meeting classmates on the street for the reunion; some were dressed formally, some in business suits, others in sports outfits, and still others in casual lounging wear. My favorite character in that dream, an unidentified female, stood chatting with others wearing a multicolored bikini and high-heeled shoes! In this dream I'm having such fun participating that I have no notion of nor interest in my outfit.

Let's examine the all-too-common complaint of women: "I haven't got a thing to wear!" Understanding the metaphor of this dream issue is extremely important. To have nothing to wear, from a commonly accepted symbology, is to be void of persona or personal identity or role within a situation.

Clearly I lacked an acceptable sense of self during the early part of this series, which occurred between the ages of twenty and forty. During those years, like most people carving out physical security by holding down busy and demanding jobs, I tended to the accepted dictates of society. I developed a variety of careers within the field of education, got married, bought a house, traveled, began drinking alcoholically, ate compulsively, divorced, engaged in melodramatic love affairs, fell deeply in love, and played uproar most of the time. In short, I lived a pretty normal, unhealthy, extroverted life.

All this time I was devoted to understanding how humans operated, and thus continued the direction set for me in college by my most influential professor and friend, S.I. Hayakawa. In Carmel, I studied with transactional psychiatrist Eric Berne and associates. Those connections increased my awareness of human transactions as well as family and cultural scripts, those usually unconscious patterns which often dictate human behavior.

But clearly all this outer development and activity were not meeting the needs of my inner self nor of my soul. Thus I was constantly searching for a missing person until the Eagle Dream catapulted me into a totally different realm of human experience.

Aminah Raheem says it this way in her book, *Soul Return:* "We may work psychologically with the personality and never integrate the essential nature and purpose of the whole person—including all the promptings of the soul and body, with their seemingly limitless strivings for wholeness." It now seems to me that, until the Eagle Dream, my ego had been going in directions abhorrent to an all-encompassing and evolving inner self. That which I could potentially become was locked in a gossamer web of awesome power. As the dreams continued, psyche addressed the needs of that self to *reunite* with its true power. Victor Biento, the person sought in my reunion dreams, is my inner guide, always pointing out which strand of the web must be severed next.

INNER EXPLORATION
Metaphor

- Identifying the metaphors in dreams helps clarify something unknown by comparing it to something familiar. This process saves us from the common mistake of literalizing the dream.

- We can think of the metaphor as providing a bridge, an *as if* bridge from image to meaning. For example, consider the image (from this chapter) of the unidentified female at the reunion wearing a multicolored bikini and high-heeled shoes. To me it seems *as if* she has no problems with the issue of dress (persona) or exposure (bikini) that so plagued dream ego throughout the series. Thus, the meaning conveyed to me was one of casual self-acceptance.

- A dream image of a charging dog baring its teeth creates many possibilities: "It is as if something ferocious wants to get me," or "I need to see a determined way of biting through something" or "Perhaps some powerfully protective force wants to get hold of me." What other metaphors come to you?

- Imagine a dream image of an ascending elevator. Use this model to access the metaphor: "It's as if I am being lifted effortlessly to a higher place (state of consciousness? mood? status?) without needing to use my own effort, resources, personal power." How would it be different if you were trudging up a long flight of stairs?

- Examine a recent dream scene for the metaphoric feeling. See how this facet of the dream brings clarity to the entire piece. You will experience a sense of rightness when you have found the right metaphor.

- The locality in a dream may metaphorically represent a *state of consciousness or psychic space*. To look at a dream locality or setting in this way ask, "What is it (like) to live in (Manhattan)? For some, the metaphor might be to live in a state of high excitement with many options. For others, Manhattan could represent a state of consciousness which is chaotic and dangerous. Someone else might see it as a place, or way of living, that abounds with creative and economic potential.

CHAPTER FOUR

Victor
Dream Mystery from the Past

If we do not claim the soul's power on our own behalf, we become its victims. We suffer our emotions rather than feel them working for us. We hold our thoughts and passions inward, disconnecting them from life, and then they stir up trouble within, making us feel profoundly unsettled or, it seems, turning into illness.

Thomas Moore, *Care of the Soul*

Interpreting and understanding dreams is a process of reclaiming or recognizing as parts of ourselves the characteristics, thoughts, and feelings that we have projected onto other characters on our dream screen.

Gayle Delaney, *Breakthrough Dreaming*

The Eagle Dream drove me to continuously examine and study my inner process—my thoughts and feelings as well as nightly dreams, daytime fantasies, and meditation images. I considered every dream a piece of data that might help explain the compelling mysterious creation of the Eagle Dream. I was determined to understand why it had impacted me so powerfully.

I quickly filled dream journals with an outpouring of material covering, it seemed, all aspects of my present and former life. Every element of my personality was exposed and examined in as many as fifteen dream scenes in a single night. Hundreds of fascinating characters roamed around or charged across my dream screen. Though most were commonplace folk or people I knew, many seemed mythic, larger than life. None of the dream characters intrigued me more than Victor Biento, the person I so desperately needed to find at the reunion dreams.

Finally, after many years of fascination with this character, I set aside a couple of weeks in 1991 to pull together and study the Victor Biento dreams. I hoped that seeing the dreams as a unit would reveal the significance of this tenacious dream force.

The Victor Biento Dream Series (1980–1996)

As this project began all I recalled about Victor was his vague existence in my long ago past. He was a kid from my high school graduating class. To say that I *knew* him in high school is imprecise. As far as my memory allows, we rarely talked, had no important contact and were definitely not involved in any significant fashion. Yet, as we will see, for over thirty-six years my psyche has presented Victor Biento as someone of supreme importance to my dreaming self.

During my first *research vacation* I plowed through fifteen dream journals, searching for dreams containing the Victor Biento character. Since I was unsure when they had begun, I was amazed to discover that the first dream in this series occurred five months after the Eagle Dream (May, 1980). I doubt I will ever forget the intense physical shock that charged through me as I read and glimpsed the importance of this dream, years after it was first given:

Making Love to Dying
Victor Biento   OCTOBER 10, 1980

I'm walking on the platform of a subway. A little girl is with me. In front of me I see someone who looks just like Victor Biento. I'm sure it is him and I smile broadly. He sees me, turns around, looks over the other people, and then begins to follow us. I stop, waiting for him to reach me. When we are finally united, I take his face in my hands and kiss him passionately. Together we remember our former connection. We make love, but Vic seems very sad all this time and I guess that he is very ill. I fear that he has cancer and is dying. I awake with the feeling of grief.

At the time I had this dream, I shared it with no one, nor did I work with it myself. Even though I recorded the dream, it didn't make its way into my conscious mind. It may have made no difference at that time for I was unable to grasp the meaning of my many dreams of trapped and dying people and animals. Although I felt the grief within my dreams, my conscious self remained shrouded in the protection of denial, emotionally detached and unaware despite intense physical distress.

I began to move through the maze of denial when I realized that the Eagle Dream was not a nightmare despite the hysterical response it caused within me. The overwhelming affect of the dream was not fear but grief. Each time

I replayed the Eagle Dream, a frequent exercise for many years, the over-whelming feeling of grief blasted forth when I looked into the eyes of the captured eagle. I began to realize that a similar gut twisting occurs when I observe the wasted lives of lethargic, caged animals in a zoo, pet store, or circus. It is triggered again at the sight of an addict with zombie eyes or people who have had the spirit whipped out of them through some form of abuse.

Contemplating the eagle's eyes reminded me that during my mother's catatonic bouts she disappeared, leaving me alone to search for any sign of presence in her blank eyes. Staring into all these types of soulless eyes evokes a terrible sense of loss. Grief. What better way for psyche to trigger my own awareness of a life that had become, at a deep level, so desperately ensnared?

When I look back on the time of the Eagle Dream I am amazed that I could so thoroughly have lost myself without noticing. When asked why I had such a griefmare then, I was truly puzzled. I thought I was coping with my mysterious illnesses and the precariousness of my long-term love relationship. Despite outbursts of emotional instability, multiple weekly nightmares, and physical and relational disintegration, I was able to deny my very troubled awake reality.

Even the probable death of dream Victor did not alert me then. Today the clarity provided by hindsight allows me to validate an interesting speculation by Jeremy Taylor in *Where People Fly and Water Runs Uphill*: "From a symbolic point of view cancer is a metaphoric expression of life energies finding inappropriate, self-destructive expression." Taylor suggests that it may be useful to think of dream cancer as a symbol of "the revenge of the suppressed, unlived life." This kind of dream warning becomes important when "the natural energies of growth and creative development manifest themselves in dangerous and disproportionate ways, in part at least because they have not been able to find expression in healthy, balanced and integrated ways." My conscious self could not recognize my physical and psychological danger but my dreamer was consistently shouting warnings of the truth.

Shortly after the Eagle Dream, I read a statement which caused me to sob spontaneously, something which always startles me and alerts me to the need for close attention. This, from Rollo May: "When a person denies his potentialities, fails to fulfull them, his condition is guilt." This truth charged through my body, striking raw nerves from head to toe. I think the denial of potential is what Jeremy Taylor means by "healthy and appropriate channels of growth" being blocked, thus causing serious dysfunction in the body—something I was to live with for a total of seventeen years.

I am now convinced that the Victor Biento character has appeared, in part, as an indicator of the condition of a vital life force. In 1980, although my conscious self was unaware of it, this life force was definitely suppressed and unlived, and a powerful energy was caught in the fine strands of potent, deadly beliefs and behaviors which held me captive. What more appropriate emotional reaction could attend this realization than grief?

What is the connection between the imprisoned eagle and dying Victor Biento? What is the significance of this dream character? Where did he come from? What is he doing in my dreams—prodding, poking, guiding, puzzling, and irritating me for over thirty-five years? These are the questions that demanded answers as I began to research the Victor Biento dreams.

INNER EXPLORATION
Griefmares

• Are you aware of dreams you could categorize as griefmares? If you recall any or can find them in your journal, write a synopsis of each piece like this:

This is the dream of a person who is grieving about _____

_____

In an easy, free, associative style, write what comes to mind in response to the above sentence. Does the dream provide any suggestions for dealing with the grief?

• Have you noticed any dream characters who seem very unhealthy or in a stage of dying? (Often animals are shown this way in dreams.) If you ascribe five adjectives to the character you may more clearly see what is in danger or dying or what, in fact, needs to die.

• If you awake from a dream feeling threatened, frightened or depressed, check to see whether the dream has created this mood. If so, why would it be useful to your healing and wholeness to feel these emotions?

• Is this a warning dream? If so, is your conscious self being urged into awareness, action, or redecision?

CHAPTER FIVE

The Escape Begins
Connecting to the Rebel

Recurrent dreams, particularly recurrent dreams with particularly strong affect, often turn out to be concise metaphoric statements of as-yet-unfulfilled aspects of the dreamer's fundamental "life task," or the deepest value conflict in his/her life, not just in the moment, but over the entire span of time during which the dream has been recurring.

Jeremy Taylor,
Where People Fly and Water Runs Uphill

Viewing the entrapped Eagle provided me with undeniably powerful motivation to change my life. As I pursued the studies that helped me understand this phenomenal dream experience, I entered into forms of therapy and healing that I had previously glimpsed only from afar. Each experience challenged my former belief systems about the functioning of the world and my part in it. Incessant dizziness, one symptom of my many undiagnosed physical ailments, intensified as my mind spun with new paradigms and personal experiences.

My behavior was undergoing dramatic change, both with and seemingly without my willing consent. A diagnosis of hypoglycemia at the onset of my physical problems had forced me to abstain from alcohol, thus halting my steady progression into alcoholism. Seven years later, after quitting smoking, I joined a recovery program for compulsive eating. Though I had long proudly described myself as a "militant" (and obnoxious) atheist, this program of recovery provided a spiritual perspective I had never envisioned. Because of a wide variety of powerful, nonrational experiences since the Eagle Dream, I surprised myself by comfortably embracing a profound level of spirituality. I opened my mind to the possibility that a nonrational happening, an intuitive awareness, a decision resulting from active imagination or meditation or a dream could be, indeed *was*, as valid as any knowing achieved through my five senses or through rational channels. The deadening, fearful beliefs and principles of my past were slowly replaced by a life-supporting philosophy accompanied by the means for practical application provided by my recovery program.

In her book *The Vein of Gold*, Julia Cameron perfectly describes what I was learning during this transformational time:

> As long as we remain closed to the possibility of spiritual help in our unfolding, we are choosing to operate off the battery pack of our limited resources. When we open to spiritual assistance—however tentatively, however experimentally—we tap into unlimited supply. No

longer restricted by the circumstances of our birth (or our current life, for that matter), we are able to receive sustenance, guidance, and even material resources that support our dreams and our flowering.

This spiritual unfolding was the point at which the despair I experienced after the Eagle Dream began to melt, one frozen block at a time.

Six months after consciously shifting my commitment from ego-dominated control to a spiritually directed life, I finally met the dream character for whom I had been searching for more than twenty years. Is it too big a stretch to suggest this *when/then*, as James Hillman terms this dynamic in dreams? *When* I have taken a major step into recovery and a spiritual perspective of life, *then* I finally connect with the sought-after energy? This vital life force? Here's the simple dream.

Recognition at Last   JANUARY 16, 1984

I'm attending a high school reunion. As I enter a room I see many kids from my class sitting and chatting. I feel very excited about seeing the person I've been looking for all these years. Will he be here? I look around and see the back of his head across the room. I know him instantly. It's Vic Biento. I'm thrilled!

My journal notes nothing more than the dream. Apparently the thrill of seeing Victor in the dream did not transfer into my conscious awareness. Even the act of writing Victor's name did not bring the person, Victor, into my consciousness. It took seven months and the two following dreams to move him from the dream depths into cognizance.

Remember that as the Victor Series first began unfolding, I was unaware of the value of studying dreams with repeating symbols. I was not yet charting a path from "Victor" in one dream to "Vic" in the next. Without acknowledging the potency of a dream series, I could not bridge it to cognition. The series worked me, but I did not work the series.

It now seems impossible that I wasn't compelled to celebrate the *Recognition at Last* dream as a resolution to the more than twenty-year reunion search. Today I would honor such a major dream event by gathering others to create a celebration ritual. And I would surely call the high school friend with whom I had shared the Reunion Series. An accomplishment in the dream world warrants commemoration as much as a success in the awake realm.

In August of the same year I received this dream.

Taming the Rebel/
Teaching the Rebel   AUGUST 28, 1984

I'm teaching Vic Biento to read. He is allowed to be in my class because I'm so good with rebellious children. I'm sad for him because he doesn't know anything about anything. However, he wants to read about history. I become excited when he sees pictures of men in wigs and identifies them rightly as Tories, men of the British Parliament. I therefore realize he knows more than is obvious.

Again, I paid little attention to this piece when I originally wrote it. As with many of the dreams that follow in this long series, I had to work with this later as a "cold" dream, one with which the person I was at the time I dreamed it could not cooperate. But to understand the steps laid down by psyche, there is no choice but to analyze with the skills I now possess, much as a detective would study clues from a long-ago crime without the aid of the victim. What did psyche want me to see, to know, to do, to be, dream after dream, that might help repair a physically ill body, an emotionally battered, grief-stricken self?

If every dream can be considered one stepping stone on the path to wellness, to wholeness, why was it important for me in 1984 to tame and teach a *rebel* who wants to know *his story* (history)? We know now that an important energy (Victor) had been reactivated and needed the cooperation of dream ego in order to learn. Since teaching and learning are two sides of the same process, I, the conscious self, will learn as well. This learning will soon return to the vital theme of rebellion.

At the time of this and the following dream, four years after the Eagle Dream, my outer and inner life had begun to change dramatically. Though I was discovering definite patterns in my dream journals, I had not yet consciously connected to the character named Victor. I had dutifully written the messages from my psyche but I had yet to transfer the dream learning to the conscious realm. In September 1984, the day had finally come for this connection to be made.

September can be extremely hot in Central California. On this particular day, intense heat had banished the fog from my coastal town, creating unusually clear, dry weather from early morning to dusk. Thus, I was sitting outside writing my dreams from that morning.

Embracing the Orphan   SEPTEMBER 4, 1984

Vic Biento is a student in my class. He's being very cooperative and cuddly. I'm going to take him home because he has been displaced and does not live with his parents. I am saddened by his orphan status.

Vic follows me into the coed restroom at school. It consists of toilets and showers mixed together. Newly under construction, it is disorganized, ill-planned. When finished, I leave the toilet unflushed to wash my hands. The new school principal teases me about his need to flush for me.

After writing the dream I read it to see what associations would surface. Then I closed my eyes to let my face soak up the sun of the glorious day.

I recalled the dream of a week before and checked my journal. Sure enough, there was the *Taming the Rebel/Teaching the Rebel* dream, and that character named Victor Biento. I saw that progress had been made because the dream rebel had become cooperative and intimate. He needed teaching and nurturing, a home. He needed to stay with me as I released old toxins. The *new principle* of my life (expanding and shifting paradigms) had to *flush away* the old processed, toxic material.

I chuckled at this representation and then reflected again on the name of this character who had moved into my dream house. Suddenly I was zapped by an undeniable *body hit*. The hair on the back of my neck stood up as the *zing* coursed through me, announcing that something vital had happened which demanded concentrated attention. Like chasing feathers in a strong wind I could *almost* catch images of an actual person named Victor! The questions started. Was this Victor character someone from my past? "What's going on here?" I said aloud to the Monarch butterflies resting on my hedge. "Who is this Vic guy?"

Completely unsure of his reality, I felt fuzzy and doubtful, but so intrigued that I decided to check my high school annuals for a name and picture that matched my dream character.

For some reason this decision scared me. Feeling tense, I plowed through an outdoor shed which held the few remaining items from my past. Finding the annuals was quite a surprise, as I had divested myself of most sentimental claptrap years before. But there they were and there he was, a handsome young man I could barely recall as I eagerly examined his face. He played hockey, I read. Yes, I could vaguely remember that. But who was this guy and why had he invaded my dreams?

Memories floated to the surface. He was the class *rebel*, wasn't he? Yes, I began to remember. He was the *rebellious* charmer who frequently played hooky or arrived late to class but was spared consequences by teasing and charming the teacher. But what was "he" doing in my dreams? Unprepared for such questions then, my head reeled.

Today I experience the brilliance of my dream life with the same awe as watching a skilled Navajo weaver. It is said that the Navajo are taught to weave by Spider Woman, who provides an innate sense of design and the meticulous labor necessary to weave an intricate rug without aid of pattern. So, it seems, does psyche weave one strand at a time, exposing the truths we need to see in order to live an authentic life rather than a scripted one. It feels to me as if this internal force sees the whole piece, but we can grasp it only one strand at a time, one dream at a time.

Standing in the hot, dark storage shed, surrounded by spiders and dust, I began the weaving process that continues to this day. In 1984, the loom had been strung with three Victor dreams, the only dreams about him in my awareness at that time. Had I been able to discern the pattern, I would have woven the three dreams like this: I had finally made contact with a force vital to my life, an essence with which I had been seeking *reunion* for twenty years. I needed to recognize the importance of establishing a relationship between me and this energy described as rebellious, orphaned, illiterate, without knowledge of history (his story).

Reflecting upon what Victor *did* know, the *Tories of the British Parliament*, took me to two different yet similar historical perspectives: I thought of the Tories from both my American and Irish heritages. In both cases, I envisioned a struggle against a very old, controlling, repressive, conservative structure opposed to anything new. Looking in the dictionary added an appreciation of opposites, for the word Tory was defined there as "an Irishman who, dispossessed by the British, in the mid-seventeenth century became a bandit!" In other words, Victor, the one for whom I had been searching for more than twenty years at this time, knew about both the repressors *and* the rebels! The brilliance of a symbol such as this one always causes me to marvel at the psyche's meticulous ability for precision far beyond the conscious self's skills.

If I was to overcome the problems that beset me at that time, I *had to* acknowledge the domination of an inner ruling force which was determined to maintain allegiance to the Old World and its Tories. I envisioned a rigid man in black robes looking ridiculous under his precariously perched stark white wig. Indeed, my loyalty to a *black-and-white*, either/or kind of thinking (my way or the highway, no possibility of compromise) had created much of the stress that resulted in my myriad physical challenges. Tired of repression, an unconscious Irish-rebel force would frequently kick in and fight against this dictating power. One way of being was no better than the other. Neither compliance nor flagrant rebellion produced the deep inner peace I needed in order to heal.

I desperately yearned for a gently loving, guiding force to rescue me from this seesaw of the controlling/rebelling dynamic. I needed an enlightened ruling dynamic, a new pair of inner parents. Then my conscious self would be able to parent this orphaned Victor energy which needed a home. Two months after I "embraced the orphan," I was thrilled by the last dream in the Plants Needing Care series presented in Chapter Two. I was clearly working on parenting and nurturing from more than one perspective.

There is another dynamic of the orphan to be explored here. In *The Little Book on the Human Shadow*, Robert Bly suggests that any part of us that we have abandoned in order to be acceptable and safe is *orphaned*. We kick these real parts of ourselves out on the streets, so to speak, disallowing them a home within us. Clearly it was time for me to welcome Victor, the abandoned rebel, into my heart and home.

There were only three Victor dreams in 1984, but each of them was potent. Psyche had given me all I could handle. The tasks of reuniting, taming and teaching, embracing and nurturing had been established. And so I did not hear from Victor Biento for four more years.

INNER EXPLORATION
Orphan/Shadow

- The chances are pretty good that you have orphaned parts of yourself, of your potential. What ways of being or doing have no place in your home?

- The orphaned or shadow aspects of our wholeness often show up in intense anger or judgment about another. You may find it useful to identify several people you really dislike, describe them, identify the particularly irritating aspects of their personality and then ask yourself this question:

  How am I like the person I'm describing? (This is called owning the shadow.) If this question is not fruitful, consider asking close friends or family if they see you as similar to person you are considering. (It's hard to see in the shadows.)

- If I am not at all like this upsetting person, do I need to integrate some of his/her characteristics despite my bias against them? (Have I disowned something I need?)

- You will discover that your emotional charge around another person will diminish after you have done this work. They will not have changed but your response to them will be different. This way you can be assured that you have welcomed some orphaned parts of yourself.

- While recording your next few dreams, look for dream characters who really upset or threaten you. See whether they fit into the shadow or orphaned category. If so, consider ways to begin to honor and enliven what is missing from your conscious being.

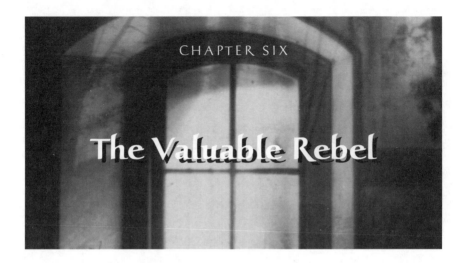

CHAPTER SIX

The Valuable Rebel

Like the god Janus, the rebel faces in two directions, negating the old in order to affirm a vision of the new. Thus the rebel is a challenger of authority; a rude iconoclast; an impudent breaker of taboos; a devotee of the sacred "no"; a destroyer of structures that have become claustrophobic, repressive. At the same time, the rebel is a dreamer; a romantic; a visionary; a creator of hope for a new order.

Sam Keen,
The Passionate Life: Stages of Loving

From the beginning of my commitment to dreamwork I often have been surprised by the issues, experiences, and feelings my dreamer has presented to my awake self. Frequently, at first glance, I do not consider significant the plot chosen by psyche. However, I have learned to trust the need to attend to the dreams' choices.

During my first intense years of dream study, my inner spotlight illuminated many unconscious beliefs and behaviors responsible for the physical and emotional problems that plagued me. As I studied each of these dreams, I began to realize that life was living me, that unrecognized patterns repeated without my input, and that I was victimized by what I did not examine.

Why did the first Victor dreams urge me to examine the role of rebel? Following psyche's focus led to many levels, literal and symbolic, inner and outer, actual and philosophical. I have since come to realize that, in a very real sense, investigating a dream is an act of rebellion against the past, our awake ego, and the roles that we play within our familial and cultural scripts. The past we lived and the future which springs from it both are challenged by an inner force that forever urges us to evolve. This evolution invariably causes us to rebel against our yesterdays in order to newly imagine tomorrow. This is not only an act of rebellion against the forces in power today; it is a revolution against the inner and outer energies that, in my case, would otherwise have controlled my future through fear, addiction, depression, and other destructive patterns.

And so, during the four years when dream Victor, the inner rebel, was silent, my outer rebel was challenging the beliefs of the collective and of my family history in every aspect of life. Shifting from a hardcore atheistic life perspective was a great rebellion against the strictly rational model I had worshipped previously. These years brought an ever-deepening commitment to the philosophy and guidelines of my chosen recovery program, which allowed me to feel my first sense of deep inner peace. I embraced the wildly alien notion that I could be addiction-free, peaceful, and happy if I released my former ways of trying to control the world. I began to see and experience the unfolding of a joyful, harmless, and helpful life as I listened to and heeded the guidance of parts of myself besides the conscious ego programmed by the past. I learned to value the perspectives of dream characters which differed from dream ego's viewpoint. I consciously rebelled against the fearmongering perpetrated by all forms of mass media. I searched for and embraced any concept that allowed me to experience inner peace without the numbing effects of addictions.

As one amazing life-affirming experience complemented another I was forced to relinquish the steadfast, unchallenged rule that dictated that my five senses and my intellect were the only reliable sources of valid information. Surprising guidance often arrived in a dream. Meditation and active imagination experiences (like the one with my therapist after the Eagle Dream described in Chapter Two) revealed dimensions of my personal reality I had never before recognized. By activating these abilities of the invisible world, I learned that I was able to meet the needs of the frantic little girl who lived inside me *without* manipulating the world. A deeply embedded shaming, blaming, guilting inner voice had no power when held in the light of my newly forming consciousness, enhanced by my spiritual and dream studies. As the next Victor dream shows, I was changing dramatically and learning to accept and love myself for the first time in my life.

Joyful Reunion   JUNE 27, 1988

I enter the room of the high school reunion. I feel energetic and am not at all shy. Everyone looks at me and some say, "Hi, Kathleen." I wonder how they know I'm using that name now. I'm delighted they recognize me as Kathleen despite my aging.

*I demand, playfully, to know where Vic is, not really
expecting him to be there. However, people move aside and
he shyly pokes his head around and waves. I surprise myself
by announcing, "I've always admired Vic for his unorthodox
view of the world and his quiet rebellious nature." He grins.*

Being referred to as *Kathleen* by the others in this dream highlights an
important change in identity for dream ego. Shortly before the Eagle Dream
I had decided to exchange the diminutive form of my name, Kathy, for my
"real" name, Kathleen. This decision grew out of my determination to develop
a different personality, to grow up, to *age*. *Kathy* was the person who existed
before the Eagle Dream; *Kathleen* represented the transforming individual
devoted to dreamwork and to physical and psycho-spiritual transformation.
Dreams often identify such transformation, as acknowledged by Rossi in
Dreams and Personality: "Words, messages, or any other form of *characterization*
of one's self in a dream are usually important aspects of personality that may be
in a *process of change*."

The feeling within the dream of high energy and a lack of shyness were
foreign to the girl/woman named Kathy. That person, from early childhood,
had been painfully shy, often depressed, usually physically lethargic, and
despite heroic attempts to play the extroverted role was rarely joyful in a gathering. My high school years of family and personal trauma intensified all of
these traits. During that time my father's uninsured business was burned out,
causing financial devastation and the loss of our family home. Unable to afford
feed and pasture, I was forced to sell the beloved old horse I had bought with
my babysitting earnings. Constant worry about my mother's mental and physical breakdowns resulted in chronic insomnia, which badly affected my ability
to focus. Poor grades pushed my already challenged self-concept into depths of
despair and hopelessness. Always embarrassed by the circumstances of my family, I felt completely unable to keep up with my peers—financially, scholastically,

or socially. Vivid scenes of being laughed at and talked about behind my back haunted me for years. But this dream, wherein I can actually *see* that which I have been seeking for so long—*Victor*—shows an accepted, joyful, energized, and bold individual. At least within the dream realm progress is being made.

I have found that to experience acceptance within a dream indicates that change has been integrated at a significantly deep level. Manifesting changes in the awake world as the result of consciously embracing new beliefs and attitudes can be a function of compliance or pretense, an "acting as if" until a fundamental alteration occurs. When deep inner change is reflected in dreams, I trust it will manifest in the awake world as well.

Activating a profound change invites something else to follow, a kind of cause-and-effect dynamic, a *when/then*. According to this dream, *when* I am finally sure of the change in my identity, *then* I can, for the first time, make contact with a seemingly paradoxical energy: Victor, the *quiet* rebel.

And at the time of this dream, changes abounded. After the Eagle Dream so altered the course of my life, I began teaching classes about the power of dreams. This eventually led to facilitating dream groups. I quickly recognized that I had never enjoyed nor benefited from any work as much as my dream activities. Thus, to allow my dream business to develop, I relinquished my stranglehold on security by exchanging my full-time public school position for half-time teaching. Finally, two weeks before the *Joyful Reunion* dream, I resigned from my teaching career to devote all of my time to professional dream work.

This *rebellion* against my former *status quo* is humorously portrayed in one of my favorite dreams, called *Cosby Over the Edge*, which occurred two days before the *Joyful Reunion* dream. In the Cosby dream, I'm standing on the edge of a *twenty-four-story* building. I see Bill Cosby on the roof of the building across the street. He waves and *jumps over the edge* as I watch in horror. I look down to the street, feeling dizzy from the height, and see a rescue service holding a net to catch him. From my perspective it looks like a hanky. I'm sure he will miss it and be killed. But no! He lands in the middle, gracefully somersaults onto the sidewalk, looks up at me flashing the high-sign that everything is fine!

Why a twenty-four-story building? Exactly the number of years I had taught! Why Bill Cosby? He's long been a role model as a multi-talented entertainer and teacher. At the time of this dream his weekly television show was exposing Americans of all races to a healthy, light-hearted parenting style. (Remember the need to parent Victor, the "orphan," in 1984.)

In addition, I think of Cosby as the first successful Black entertainer and teacher on television. One part of me felt that my ability to achieve success in my new career would be as unique as Cosby's. Why does he need to jump? I described my decision to leave teaching as a *leap of faith* in the inner spiritual process which had begun with the Eagle Dream!

I awoke from this dream with a great sense of joy and security. I profoundly needed both because my conscious self could easily panic during this transition time. A major move away from financial security, from the status quo, is bound to be threatening. This is one of those times when I counted heavily on dreams to tell the whole truth by providing a perspective my awake self could not envision. This dream delivered!

And so, supported by my dreams and my spiritual practices, I committed daily acts of quiet rebellion. My newly acquired sense of self and of the world provided the courage necessary to break the life-threatening strands of the web by extricating me from a career that was no longer fulfilling. In this and many other ways I was leaping off the edges of the past and landing in an entirely new life. It appears that the quiet rebel with an unorthodox world view was serving me well.

INNER EXPLORATION
Dream Dialogue

- Check your dream journal for statements, usually written in quotations, that describe or define yourself. Does this characterization of yourself describe important aspects of your personality that may be in a process of change?

- Pay special attention to dreams in which dream ego is different from your sense of your awake self. Is the dream change one you value? Does it show growth in an area where you have been applying conscious energy? Does the change represent either a ridiculous inflation or deflation of the you with which you and others are familiar?

- Sometimes dream ego takes a very different form from your awake identity. You may be a different sex, an alien, a pioneer crossing the prairie, or the President of Argentina. Work each identity metaphorically and see what happens.

- Occasionally a dream presents a very specific statement that must be written as a quotation. It's as if we have been taking dictation while sleeping. Most dreamers are intrigued with such statements. Some dreamers feel a sense of the numinous while working with these quotations. Pay special attention to such inner dialogue. Share it with others. These little jewels often have profound value.

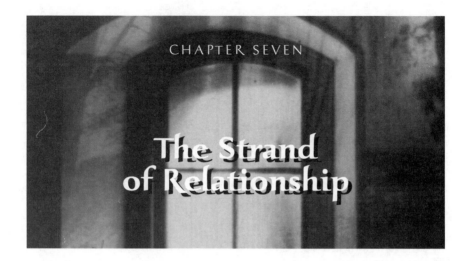

CHAPTER SEVEN

The Strand of Relationship

The need for individual development does not invalidate relationship. Only separated beings can relate. Unless there is individual development on the part of two people, true relationship cannot occur. Instead, a state of mutual identification develops that blunts the psychological development of both partners.

John Sanford, *The Invisible Partner*

As the Reunion series continued, I saw that the dream confronted all facets of my life. The next dream in the series wrangles with the issue of relationships.

Amethyst Collie   JULY 1, 1988

I see Victor Biento sitting on the beach facing the ocean. Arms wrapped around his legs, he looks peaceful but lonely. I'm thrilled to see him and enthusiastically run toward him. On my way I pick up an amethyst figurine carved by the ocean into the shape of a collie dog. This I shyly and tenderly offer to Vic. He loves but sadly rejects it. I then find a statue that he does accept but I can't recall what it is.

Later I explain to someone that the reason for the rejection is that care of a dog is too demanding at this time.

To understand this dream we must understand the significance of the collie dog. This was the second time that symbol had emerged since 1980. Remember that, following the Eagle Dream, I undertook an active imagination in which the eagle attempted to escape its web by transforming into a collie:

As I focused on the agony of the eagle, she transformed into a tricolored collie dog, jumped out of the web and ran toward me, wagging her tail. "NO!" I screamed. "NO! Get back in the web until you can get out on your own power!"

A tricolored collie, named Mollie, was my worshipped pet and constant companion during three very difficult teenage years. She trotted along beside me as I trained my spooky old quarter horse. Each time I was thrown to the ground, Molly was there to lick my face and soothe my pride. Together we quietly roamed the mountain, encountering wildcats, deer, and snakes. In a chaotic household she was the only even-tempered, constantly loving creature. She was the family protector and caretaker, even adopting a litter of abandoned kittens and nurturing them into maturity. My mother often described her as a truly *selfless* animal whose only purpose in life was caring for others. Indeed, Molly would wake me in the morning and pull me from bed to feed my horse when his whinnies did not rouse me. Although I adored this collie dog she was not an acceptable substitute for the eagle in the web. Nor was what she represented healthy for me at the time of the Amethyst Collie dream.

As I committed to a full-time dreamwork and counseling career, I needed to expand the healing seen in the Plant Series by rejecting the role of the overly responsible caretaker. Thus, Victor, the quietly rebellious masculine energy I had been searching for all these years, could not accept the carved *amethyst collie dog* at this time. (It's interesting to note that amethyst is said to be beneficial in curing addictions.) The important inner rebel is not yet healed enough to accept the role of *the selfless one*.

That understanding, though true and important, is not inclusive enough for the symbol of the collie, for it excludes the adoring, unconditionally loving relationship aspect offered by Mollie and so important for rich human living. At another level, the lonely sadness with which Victor rejects the collie illustrates the following decision I needed to make at the time of the dream.

A few months before this dream I had become interested in Wayne, a bright, light-hearted, and attractive man. After dating awhile, I contemplated my readiness for a sexual relationship. Due to previous takeovers by the romantic archetype, I was wary of that powerful force which creates sublime insanity from adolesence through old age. I was also vibrantly aware that the web which entrapped the eagle perfectly describes unconscious relationships, each as beautiful as it is deadly.

For four years preceding this dream I had chosen to remain free from romantic relationships, believing them to be a distraction and a drain I was not strong enough to handle. For the most part, I was clear that abstinence from this potentially addicting dynamic was essential for my physical, emotional, and spiritual survival. In retrospect I am sure that was a valid decision.

Reflecting upon Victor in this dream allowed me to acknowledge that I was, at times, both *lonely* and *sad* as a result of my decision. However, I no longer followed the promptings of my awake self, who saw something, wanted it, and manipulated the world to get it. Instead I was, and still am, deeply determined to make decisions only after contemplation with my *ocean*, a symbol of the original source of life as well as the collective unconscious. The contemplative rebel on the beach, the vital life force so important to my inner journey, continued to be clear as well; he was not ready to accept the *collie dog* and the type of relationship that indicated. The dream allowed me to see that I was still too likely to revert to that tail-wagging, determined-to-please, caretaking energy from my less conscious past.

One of my favorite dreams substantiated Victor's decision on the beach. Perhaps since the rejection came from Victor instead of dream ego, I was not totally convinced that romance was not yet a healthy decision. To be sure Victor was right, I incubated (consciously requested) a dream about Wayne, the above-mentioned friend. Because one part of me wanted an intimate, sexual relationship, I challenged my dreamer for another perspective. (Incubation is a very *real* way to go to the ocean [the unconscious] to contemplate a situation.)

The first REM cycle of the night presented a delightful dream showing Wayne and me at Niagara Falls on the lovely rose garden walk. I'm having the time of my life being *pushed in a wheelchair* by my adoring lover. I think how great it is that, without exertion, I get to see the sights while everyone else has to walk. Then the path gets very steep and I feel sorry that Wayne has to struggle so much. So I drop my feet onto the ground and pull hard with obviously healthy legs!

I awoke instantly from the dream with the message received and accepted. Had I moved into a romantic *(Niagara Falls)* relationship at that time, I would revert to the helpless dependent role *(the one in the wheelchair)* from which I was so determined to be free. In this dream we see that unconscious caretaking has two equally difficult sides.

I shared the dream with Wayne the next day. He laughed as much as I, adding what my conscious mind had not yet learned. Wayne reported that in all of his previous relationships he immediately became the rescuer/caretaker, and that he had been defined by his former wife as "smothering." In a very real sense, both Wayne and I could be seen as collie dogs. Another save by psyche!

The next chapter examines Victor's influence on inner balance and its significance in the outer realm.

INNER EXPLORATION

Dream Incubation

- During times of profound change or upset, consider incubating a dream for guidance. An hour or so before bedtime, simply write a clear statement in your dream journal, asking for clarity or direction. For example: "I request a dream that provides information about the job I am considering."

- As you prepare for bed, recall your intention. As you drift off to sleep, implant the suggestion firmly in your consciousness.

- Immediately write your dream recall throughout the night or in the morning. Work the dream in your usual fashion and then work it from the perspective of the incubated question.

- Often the view of another dream student will be helpful. To preserve your dream helper's objectivity, do not reveal the incubated question before working the dream. After you both are comfortable with the interpretive work, read the question to see how it fits with the overall work.

- It may take several nights to receive a response from psyche. Perhaps you will need to simplify your question. "Tell me what to do with my life now" may be too complex. "What is causing the anger in my relationship with Dottie?" is more likely to be helpful.

CHAPTER EIGHT

Balance

The yang-yin, Lingam-Yoni symbolism seems archetypally ingrained in our psyches, as a representation of fundamental polarity both between partners and within the individual psyche. Outgoing-indwelling, light-dark, initiating-responsive, creative-receptive, assertive-adaptive are but a few of the possible meanings which may be implied by gender images in dreams, regardless of the gender of the dreamer.

Edward C. Whitmont and Sylvia Brinton Perera,
Dreams: A Portal to the Source

Letting go versus doing, that primordial polarity of yin and yang that assumes a thousand different forms and is never exhausted. It is not that yin or yang is right, that being is better than doing—it's a question of finding the right balance, finding the natural harmony between yin and yang that the ancient Chinese called the Tao.

Ken Wilber, *Grace and Grit*

The final Victor Biento dream of 1988 shows Victor in a different and
very important light.

Hey, Vic! JULY 25, 1988

*I walk into a room and actually see Victor Biento sitting on
a chair in his inimitable laid-back style. I charge over to him
and say, "There you are! I've been looking for you for thirty
years!" He looks very surprised, baffled. I explain our dream
history and he laughs. He introduces me to his gorgeous
brunette wife and lovely daughter.*

The important part of this dream is the presence of the "wife" and
"daughter." To understand this inclusion, I ask myself how it would be different if I met only Victor, if he had no wife or daughter? Answer: This element
for which I have been searching for so long wouldn't be balanced and feeling
(wife) or reproductive *(daughter)*.

It seems to me that at the time of this dream, the "daughter" represented
my new belief system, lifestyle, and career. These had come into being as a
result of *the marriage* between my internal masculine and feminine dynamic, a
new balance I had consciously developed during my commitment to extricate
the eagle from her web.

To understand the significance of that dynamic and this dream, we must
focus on one of the most valuable dream theories in my personal work: understanding the inner dynamic of the so-called masculine and feminine principles. (These descriptors refer to principle or process and should not be
confused with gender roles. I find the terms applicable and precise, but if you
feel semantically compromised, think in terms of yin/yang, eros/logos, exter-
nal/internal, feeling/being, thinking/doing, right brain/left brain or any other

pair of opposites that brings clarity to your understanding.)

I first became fascinated by the masculine/feminine principle because many of my dreams featured unidentified male and female characters to whom I could not relate or associate. When I learned of Carl Jung's understanding of these energies, I began a conscious procedure which helps me in my daily life and has been consistently helpful to clients who complain that their lives go around and around without accomplishment (unbalanced feminine), or are lived without feeling and meaning (unbalanced masculine).

Simply stated, each of us contains within us opposing or contrasting forces. Both masculine and feminine types of energy are essential to our human process. These terms attempt to differentiate between two contrasting ways that all humans, both males and females, have of operating in and processing the world. Each is vital for a well-lived, whole life. Neither is good or bad. *Both* are necessary.

Having *conscious* access to these two energies by understanding when each is most useful consistently allows me choices which enhance the flow of my life. These choices help to repair the damage done by the Tory controllers known by Victor the Orphan (Chapter 5). When that domineering force was in charge, I was either compliantly compulsively on or rebelliously totally off, either *doing* (masculine) or *being* (feminine) but I did not have the ability to choose the most helpful process. Now I can see, or be told by a dream or a friend, when I am out of whack, and I am able to make choices which create balance.

Before the Eagle Dream, for all of my adult life, I had suffered from a predominantly goal-oriented, focused, driven, compulsive energy. I had found it safer to deal with facts than feelings. I needed to control relationships and all other aspects of my world. In short, my process orientation was left-brained and masculine, with very little regard for the feminine relational, receptive, feeling mode.

Unconscious masculine perspective does not include acceptance of what is. It is not a peaceful way to proceed in the world because goals take precedence over natural unfolding. This stressful perspective sums up my life prior to dreamwork. Prior to the Eagle Dream I deliberately swam upstream searching for rocks against which to bloody my head. Thus victimized, I was able to complain bitterly about the damnable river and the obstinate rocks. But how proud I was of the scars on my forehead!

The inclusion of the feminine principle was essential at this juncture in my growth. Though vital life-giving changes had occurred following the Eagle Dream, my body was still very much distressed. Dizziness, headaches, food and environmental allergies, chronic candida, fatigue, and skin eruptions were constant problems. Learning how to nurture, to care for instead of hate, judge, and reject my body was a major challenge at this time.

The feminine aspect within includes the internal mother, the unconditional nurturing energy which cares for and provides many of the needs of the entire organism. An individual who has not been appropriately mothered as a child must learn this life-giving process as an adult. Learning how to appropriately nurture myself has been a very conscious challenge for most of my life.

Seeing that Victor is now *married* and *reproductive* brought a great deal of relief and hope. Such messages are among the greatest benefits of dreamwork, because the awake ego is the last to see the changes that are occurring. By activating the feminine energy within and wedding it to the newly contacted Victor energy, a blending had resulted, creating a beautiful and healthy "daughter," an entire new life.

I find it extremely useful to synthesize the learning from a series of dreams as the series unfolds. Applying that to the Victor dreams thus far shows a stunning movement from a dying Vic in 1980 to a reproducing Vic in 1988. By seeing the importance of quiet rebellion and an unorthodox world view and following that urging, I had embraced a previously rejected, spiritual, feminine-feeling perspective. This provided such faith in my unfolding process that I was able to leave my tenured teaching career. Devoting my life to the dream brought a great sense of personal respect, creating a new foundation for healing my severely wounded self-esteem. By working consciously to balance my masculine, goal-dominated process with receptive feeling and nurturing, I was replacing inner torment with peaceful joy.

At this point in 1988, many strands of the web had been severed, but many were still intact. Happily, the dreams continue their inexorable restructuring. The individuation process has many facets, angles, and layers, as the dreams of 1989 reveal.

Life constantly strives to bring out unique and new forms. In the very heart of the unconscious lies the deep instinct to bring about a whole, unique personality in us. Jung called this the urge to *individuation*, that is to become an undivided person, whose conscious personality is at one with the unconscious. He saw the urge to individuation as the fundamental instinct in life.

John Sanford, *Dreams and Healing*

INNER EXPLORATION

Masculine Principle

- Think of masculine energy as that which goes forth into the world, thrusts into, stays on track, is logical, linear, and goal-oriented. Now look at the characteristics, procedures, or mental processes within you. Can you accomplish short- and long-term goals? When confronted by a complex issue can you logically figure it out? Are you successful and comfortable in the world?

- Another way to understand the masculine is to consider it the doer, the part which does, the element of the self which accomplishes. Are you satisfied with these abilities within yourself?

- Check your dreams for unknown men. What characteristics do they reflect? Is one kind of character (perhaps a generic successful businessman or a handyman) repeating? Are the masculine roles in your dreams played by powerful men or wimps? What do you notice?

- People we know can represent the masculine or feminine principle. Often a woman's husband plays the role in her dreams of her animus, her inner masculine. Likewise, a man's wife can show the workings of his anima, his inner feminine aspect. To distinguish this role from the awake relationship, refer to the husband in the dream not as "Ralph" but as "the masculine." This semantic shift often objectifies and clarifies these roles.

- Questions concerning the feminine principle are at the end of the next chapter.

CHAPTER NINE

The Destructive Rebel

A person who identifies with being a rebel or nonconformist may be dominated by collective role models just as much as the person who feels compelled to conform.

Frances Vaughan,
The Inward Arc: Healing in Psychotherapy and Spirituality

When my former husband and I traveled throughout Ireland, my ancestral home, I was awestruck by the country's beauty and delighted by its warm, humorous, and poignant people. Most of all, I reveled in the ever-present rebellious Irish nature celebrated in song and story in every pub. I had long been proud to align myself with the *fighting Irish spirit* as it is celebrated in both Ireland and America. I applauded the acts of rebellious heroism intended to free a country oppressed for hundreds of years (by the *British Parliament*, of course!). However, until my dream about *Taming the Rebel, Teaching the Rebel* (Chapter 5), I did not recognize that I was operating unconsciously from that cultural script in very harmful ways.

The development of my destructive rebel probably goes beyond cultural scripting. During normal adolescence rebellion is a necessary and healthy stage. The appropriate response of nurturing parents to such rebellion assists teenagers in separating from the family. It is essential for a developing individual to feel a sense of personal power in the world. Without it we may not be able to define ourselves or to stand up for our particular values. However, during adolescence, when it was appropriate for me to act out in this way, I had to stuff these natural inclinations into a bag and hide them away. As my mother's primary caretaker, I needed to comply with the family's needs.

The single attempt at rebellion while living at home occurred when I went on a ski trip with a friend and her family. As we left town I announced, laughingly, that I was going AWOL and would surely be punished for my transgressions. I vividly recall standing in the snow, making frequent phone calls home to assure myself that mother was still alive. Not much freedom, joy, or separation in that. Thus, my rebel went underground, where it fermented and stirred up trouble for many years.

Herein lies an intriguing paradox with the rebel Victor character. I needed *to activate* the healthy rebel (to fight against repression) and *to release* an unconscious and destructive rebel (which caused harm). I needed to make contact with the rebel so that it could become conscious while healing a type of rabid energy that created internal and external chaos.

Reflecting upon the *Taming the Rebel/Teaching the Rebel* dream led me to the "good old days" when I often marched into battle with authority figures, frequently embarrassing myself with inappropriate behavior that often felt out of my control. I thought I was just doing my Irish duty of fighting the oppressors. From the perspective of others, I was a jerk who unpredictably and inappropriately flew off the handle. In the vernacular of the 1984 dream, I knew a lot about the Tories, thought I saw repressive forces everywhere, and constantly raged against them.

In my review of the past, I can applaud my rebellious nature when it served to right wrongs and to improve situations. But much of my rebellion was destructive to professional and personal relationships, expensive, and stressful. The following microwave incident was one simple, ridiculous, and all-too-common example.

After buying a microwave oven, I read the manufacturer's warning that using the same electrical outlet for the oven and refrigerator would burn out the refrigerator's condenser. Because putting the oven on another outlet was inconvenient, I made a clear decision to overlook the warning, thinking, "Those guys don't know what they're talking about. They're just trying to shove people around." Six hundred dollars and a freezer of thawed food later, the rebel was chagrined.

In those vainglorious days I was just as likely to reject directions that were verbal. When my community acquired its first sport center, I joined a body-building class and acquired an experienced trainer. He designed a program specific to my age, strength, and personal goals. Within the first hour, deciding that he didn't know what he was doing, I altered the program. In the weeks to come, anything I didn't like about the routine was categorized as another of the expert's mistakes. Needless to say, I experienced no benefit from this six-month training program.

These examples illustrate my former belief that authority figures were, at best, misinformed and usually motivated by intent to harm. Thus, I was often belligerent to those in charge. My head was filled with incessant inner dialogue of attack/defend. Perceiving myself as perennially victimized by the system, I was always ready, willing, and delighted to jump into the ring and duke it out.

I've learned to see this out-of-control rebellion in another, more instinctive way which may be true for anyone suffering with addictive behavior. After a short time in recovery I recognized that much of the inner emotional charge I felt when misusing a substance could be attributed to rebelling against an authority. Like the little girl who got away with stealing a cookie from the jar, I experienced my addictions as *getting away with something*. I realized that my recovery depended upon overcoming that rebellious inclination.

Anytime I override an inner instinctive knowing which clearly signals that I have had enough (of anything), my ego is rebelling against the authority of my body. By the same token, unless my rebel is conscious and working *with* me I am likely to ignore the inner voices which direct my spiritual journey. This rebellious energy was definitely in control when I swam upstream against the current, bashing my head against the boulders. Through dreamwork I have learned to own all parts of myself and facilitate cooperation between them. Now I know that I am the river, the rocks, and a woman with the ability to let the flow guide me. Today if I opt to boogie with white water I no longer fuss about the resultant bruises or sore muscles. Recognizing all of these facets of rebellion's down side helps me work through this "fight or surrender" conflict to peace.

One of the many diagnoses made during my seventeen years of illness was Chronic Fatigue Syndrome (CFS). Constantly and violently rebelling against life takes a major toll on the adrenals, which may have been one cause of *my* CFS. During my recovery I learned to identify and avoid both behaviors and beliefs which unnecessarily drained my energy. The following dream, the first Victor dream of 1989, shows a shift away from the destructive rebel.

Respectable Rebel   JUNE 13, 1989

I'm back in my home town again for another reunion. I have lots of energy and feel completely relaxed as I enjoy talking with a bunch of former classmates in a restaurant. They report changes in their lives. I, too, have news of change and excitedly share that rebellious Victor Biento is living a happy and respectable life in a beautiful old town in California.

This dream suggests that connecting to the *quiet, reflective* and now *respectable* rebel releases my own natural energy. In order to heal my body, the romantic image of the wild fighting Irish has to be replaced by a quiet, reflective force that can check in *with all parts of myself* before acting on a decision. This reflection allows an opportunity to see things differently, decreasing the probability of a knee-jerk reaction and the problems that result from it.

The theme of the healed self-image continues with this dream. It's important to see that a change has occurred from an unconscious rebellious spirit to a happy life that can be respected. By the time of this dream, my inner sense of self, my personality, and my life had changed so much that I could finally respect who I had become. This was a vast improvement from my fighting Irish days, when bravado had substituted for happiness and self-respect.

To consciously and quietly rebel without hurting myself or others was an ability I attributed to Victor. Throughout high school I had watched him do what he wanted *without* getting into trouble. With the beginning of the Victor dreams in 1984 I connected to that conscious, quiet rebel. I then was able to calmly create revolutions with my mind which allowed me to go beyond the imagination of my family and the general society into a world not yet known. I could consciously rebel against my personal behaviors and a collective mindset that limited both my potential and my future.

The guidance of Victor Biento in my dreams all these years has led me to the freedom of conscious choice, to the luxury of choosing *against* one belief in order to choose *for* a different principle. Only in this state do we, as individuals and as a collective, *truly* access our advantage over other species for whom evolution has no element of conscious choosing.

The dreams thus far have helped me achieve a more balanced life process, in part by taming an unconscious inner rebel. In contrast, the next chapter shows how the rebel was needed to repair a severely compromised physical body.

INNER EXPLORATION

Feminine Principle

- Think of feminine energy as that which is receptive, hidden, circuitous, comfortable with mystery, spiritual, feeling, and intuitive. Now look at these characteristics, procedures, or mental processes within you. Are you comfortable with mystery, with not knowing, with not needing to be in control? Can you wander around, enjoying going from activity to activity without a plan or a time limit? Do you enjoy engaging with others at a feeling level? Are you familiar with and do you trust your intuition?

- Another way to understand the feminine is to consider it the part of you that is happy to just be, exist, experience without having to do or accomplish. Are you satisfied with these abilities within yourself?

- Choose ten dreams from the past year which contain unidentified men and women. Briefly describe all the women on one sheet and all the men on another. What do you notice? Is one particular type of person appearing over and over? Which sheet shows the most power? The most feeling? The least joy or accomplishment? Are you pleased with what you see, or do you feel a need for balance?

- Consider the various roles you play in life and see where you fall on the continuum:

doing	being
controlling	allowing
thinking	feeling
initiating	responding
outgoing	indwelling

CHAPTER TEN

Changing World View

...dreams reveal the general "conception of the world" a person holds, the world view by which a person understands the total nature of his or her surrounding environment.

Calvin Hall,
The Meaning of Dreams

In the practical everyday world, growth is usually achieved throughout a process of struggle; basically a struggle to get free from the grip of the older conventional viewpoint so we can try new ways of living and experiencing. In experimenting with new ways of living and feeling we are actually creating new states of being.

Ernest Rossi,
Dreams and the Growth of Personality

ix months after the *Respectable Rebel* dream, Victor and I connect in an unexpectedly distressing way. This dream highlights the long-term illness from which I had been unable to escape and the belief system or *world view* which maintained the illness. I now see it as a pivotal dream in this transformative series. But on the night of the dream in 1989 it only added to my depression.

The Christmas season had caught me unaware, with neither the energy nor the desire to participate in the usual festivities and gift giving. For several days I had been spontaneously plagued by images from a series of dreams and nightmares which had bothered me for years. In each dream, I awake in the morning to discover that Christmas has come and gone without my participation. Every dream brings a deep sadness and sense of loss, similar to my feelings about my physical condition at the time. On this particular night, I felt that not only Christmas but all of life was passing me by. By this time, I had felt barely alive for thirteen years. A rare day of high energy, clarity, optimism, and joy was always followed by three or four days of lethargy and depression of varying degrees of severity. I had managed to continue working, pursuing my study of the dream, and nurturing a limited social life—but always with a dizzy, half-present feeling.

My strongly negative response to the following dream fit perfectly with my bah-humbug emotional state.

Helping Vic Recover from Booze
DECEMBER 18, 1989

Vic and I are together at last. I'm helping him recover from alcoholism. He looks disheveled, down-and-out, sickly, without energy.

Despite this, I'm happy to finally be with Vic and expect we'll become lovers when he's sufficiently recovered.

I'm gazing at him in fascination because his teeth are false and look like a video cassette. I suspect the teeth were lost in a hockey game. I wonder how he allows such a hideous apparatus. I'm surprised I'm still attracted to him.

This dream frightened and frustrated me. I had been sober for thirteen years, and was angry that the dream seemed to request something I had already accomplished (recovery from alcoholism). I was worried that Vic was sick, that the energy I had been seeking for so long was waning. I'd finally found this guy but suddenly he was in worse shape than I! No previous dream had pictured him in this way. The image generated the kind of inner queasiness I sometimes feel when I'm in the presence of a dying animal or person.

Before dragging my exhausted body and disgruntled mind out of bed, I wrote many questions and frustrations in my dream journal. I thought about *teeth* being that which begins the assimilation, integration, and nourishing process. I personally related to the connection between teeth and eating because of the food allergies and candida that had plagued me for thirteen years. Metaphorically, teeth either bite through issues or hang onto beliefs in the same way that dogs hang on to old bones. Teeth are intricately involved with issues of vanity and persona. That they were pictured here as a black videocassette baffled me. I was so upset by this dream and the overwhelming holiday season that I wanted to haul the covers over my head and hide under them forever.

Throwing the seduction of denial aside, I plunged into warm walking clothes and stumbled off to the beach, encouraged by recollection of the many previous occasions when my despairing mental state had shifted during a walk. The physical stimulation seems to encourage the dream to perc and release necessary information so that it can bubble to the surface. Usually these quiet walks allow me to access an inner reality which understands the dream's intent despite the dense-ness of my conscious self. As I trudged along, confused and angry, I recognized a familiar thought activated by reviewing the image of a sick and addicted dream Victor. Mentally examining his waning energy I said out loud, "No one can be counted on, ever. Not even a damn dream character!"

I caught this thought before I could file it away as truth, and recognized a deeply embedded belief: *Nothing can be trusted.* I was immediately overwhelmed by a feeling of hopelessness with the world and with my inner process as well. If *nothing* could be trusted, then my dreams and other spiritual connections were also unreliable. Since I had committed my life to trusting these forms of guid-ance, I felt panic rise from the pit of my stomach. This was immediately fol-lowed by such extreme fatigue that I doubted my ability to retrace the two-mile walk to my home.

I sat on a boulder to regain my strength. My physical eyes watched waves blasting against Pacific Grove's rocky shore while my inner sight continued to focus on a sickly Victor with his ugly, black teeth. I squirmed, trying to escape the deeply painful feeling this image generated. Suddenly the dream connected to outer reality. I recognized how my present feelings about Victor matched the despair I had felt about my illness for so many years. As I sat on that damp, wind-blown rock, I realized that these were the same feelings of hopelessness and exhaustion I had felt in childhood. Scenes of two traumatic childhood Christ-mas seasons flashed behind my eyes, forcing tears to mix with the ocean spray on my face. The repetitiveness of these feelings overwhelmed me. "My God, my entire life I've *felt* the way that Victor *looks*." I said aloud.

Immediately a rush of energy, like an electric charge, signaled that a deeply significant truth was bridging the dream to awake awareness. I *knew* that I could now access some imperative truth about the illness, its creation, and its cure. I felt that intense sense of *awe* inspired by great dreams, synchronicities, and other spiritual revelations. I recognized this as the same feeling I had experienced when I committed to extricating the eagle from the web. Though it would take many more hours to sort the rest of the dream, to move it into an intellectual awareness, on that cold December day I knew a major step had been taken. Wrapped in the warmth of deep gratitude, I trekked home energized by the power of hope and the anticipation of healing.

Over the next few days of journal writing and dream sharing with others, I realized that the *video cassette teeth* represented what I had *bitten off* from my family and culture, forever repeating a pessimistic, hopeless world view. Just as a videotape is played and replayed, so did I replay the feelings of exhaustion and despair which may have caused my mother's severe mental and physical illness and, eventually, her suicide. I became aware that the severity and length of my own chronic illness was metaphorically just as suicidal as my mother's death.

I squarely confronted the belief that *no one can be counted on.* To begin, I analytically reviewed my lifetime of relationships. This led me to see clearly that the belief was both *true* and *false.* It was certainly true from the perception of my inner little girl who had been severely wounded by unstable and untrustworthy relationships in childhood. It was less true when I recognized the natural ebb and flow of people, into and out of one another's lives, serving the needs of learning and growing. This kind of vitality, the coming and going of people in our lives, does not equate with "unreliable relationships."

Regardless of the individuals involved, I could see now that all relationships expand, contract, and transform. According to my former perception, the immature view, I could count on no one to remain *enough* the same to soothe my insecure young self; but now I was learning that this inner child's fear had resulted from *counting on the unaccountable* instead of trusting herself and her Self. Since the Eagle Dream I had been steadily learning to value, to count on, and to trust my relationship with myself. Although that *inner* relationship changed constantly, *it* could always be counted on. This realization produced a profound feeling of security.

As I wrangled with Vic needing to recover from addiction I saw that, after thirteen years of illness, *I had become addicted* to the plethora of *symptoms* which *numbed me* out, in much the same way as alcohol once had. Just as I had previously used alcohol to avoid *feeling life*, I used my illness to avoid *living life*. Anytime I was presented with a challenge or an opportunity that threatened me, my illness provided a powerful excuse to avoid participation.

The dream said that Victor had lost his teeth in a hockey game. Focusing on that statement allowed me to realize that, during my drinking years, I had played violent and exciting games (*hockey*) with others and within myself. Not only had these games replaced something natural and healthy which facilitated nourishment (*teeth*) with an ugly, negative, black persona (*video cassette*); they also were fueled by the same kind of energy I imagined was necessary to hockey players—adrenalin.

Three months before this dream I had been introduced to the phrase "addiction to adrenalin" during an unusual experience on a daily walk. (These walks were a prescription from my doctor and the only medication which seemed to provide healing.) Dragging my perennially fatigued body into the home stretch, I saw a very handsome man wearing a neck and back brace. He looked as joyless as I felt. Since we were walking the same narrow path along the rocky shore we combined our walking with talking. We stopped to watch some surfers dance with very large swells. When I commented on the danger of being so close to the rocks he responded by saying that added to the thrill. His next sentence charged through me as I recognized his truth as my own. "I should know," he said bitterly. "Being an *adrenalin addict* broke my back and destroyed my life."

Though I had never before thought of that kind of chemical dependence, I immediately identified myself as having been dependent upon the power of adrenalin most of my life. This chemical, a natural component of my perpetual fight or flight response, had created the false bravado necessary for all the melodrama and uproar I acted out.

My dream said that dream ego had to help Vic (the energy I sought and needed) *recover from addiction*. As I wove the various strands of the dream together I concluded that I needed to make a *conscious commitment* to recover from the addictive *beliefs* and *practices* that resulted in the chronic symptoms that had so long imprisoned me.

I never doubted that I *had to* heal this all-important Victor energy. It didn't seem strange to me that these significant decisions were motivated by a dream image rather than by my own reflection in a mirror! In retrospect, this dream and the decisions it prompted allowed me to move ahead, unconflicted, into deep psychological and spiritual healing. Up to this point I had bounced back and forth between traditional and mental healing models, feeling dependent upon medical doctors but never truly helped by their ministrations. Because I believed I was now dealing with the beliefs that had created the illness, I was able to proceed with a deep sense of faith in the internal healing process.

One of the many thrilling benefits of dream work is the release of energy when a previously buried truth is uncovered. New power is now available to commit to a new goal and direction. It very much feels like the soul gulps in a breath of relief, knowing that the right track has been found, leading where the soul—not the personality—wants to go. Thus it was with this dream. With a great upsurge of energy and a rededication of focus, I was able to fully participate in the Christmas season and joyfully celebrate the New Year with the following dream, the last of the Victor Biento dreams of 1989.

Washing Mounds of Dishes
while Vic Pedals   DECEMBER 30, 1989

I'm standing at a sink in a room with no walls. I'm washing someone's dishes as a result of losing a bet. Amused by the process, I am teasing and bitching about how many dishes there are for me to do. I have already loaded three dish drainers with all the dishes in the house.

I'm washing a small hand-blown glass pot. I'm intrigued as I begin to pull some material from the pot in order to clean it. It has an enormous amount of protective packing material stuffed inside. I look up and see Victor in a suit and tie, riding a bike. I surprise myself by calling to him. He dismounts and joins me. I ask if he knows anything about dreams. He answers, "I know they are important."

I then tell him I have dreamed about him for thirty years. I'm glad to see him now and tell him some of the dreams. He returns to his bike and I to the dishes.

Because the womb within the feminine is the container for life, pots and other kinds of vessels can represent the feminine. Therefore, the *hand-blown pot*, an object created with great attention and consciousness, may be the feminine principle or intuitive, spiritual process discussed earlier. In contrast, the *protective packing material* can be seen as the defensive, aggressive, harsh attitudes necessitated by my *repetitive, black* world view. To clean the consciously created life *(hand-blown glass vase)* based on faith in my inner spiritual processes, I had to remove the old protective beliefs. This new feminine process cannot be used if the old defensive patterns remain.

An example of this feminine process is trusting and following images from dreams, active imagination, and meditation. The majority of my healing has resulted from making contact with this feminine, intuitive, spiritual process. Learning to access, follow, and rely upon the *ephemeral* instead of the *material* has been my major way of healing the beliefs represented by the black videotape.

My spiritual practices have allowed me to depend upon an inner transpersonal Self which, unlike the ever-changing material world, will always be present. Accessing this dependable, life-giving source can occur only when I, the vessel, have rid myself of former defenses which block me from receiving, from being filled up. Happily, by the time of this dream, I had spent five years in spiritual study, cleaning out the old packaging. This dream substantiated that the jig was up, so to speak. I had lost a previously made bet and now had to clean up, to pay the consequences. This I was more than willing to do.

After much contemplation I wrote this in my dream journal: "I'm in an open, expanded place *(room with no walls)*. I'm *cleaning up* more than I expected. I bet on something that didn't pay off (illness?) and now must clean all former ways of nourishing. *When* I pull out the protective material from the consciously created self *(hand-blown pot)*, *then* I see the respectable *(suit and tie)* balanced *(on bike)* rebel who validates my new life's purpose and spiritual process *(the dream)*."

The *Helping Vic Recover* dream demands that dream ego be the healer. The *Mounds of Dishes* dream says that she must make a *conscious decision* to clean all that was *dished out* in family beliefs about what is needed for survival, *food*. The dreams in many of the following chapters identify these beliefs. Each belief is one strand of web that ensnared the Eagle.

This dream felt like an enormously productive and hopeful way to end the year. I recall that I insisted upon doing all the dishes at a New Year's Eve luncheon to ritualize the dream. As I washed dish after dish, cleaning and releasing the past, I marveled at the change from pessimism to optimism that these two dreams had produced. I felt deep gratitude for the release and change of energy which resulted from working with these dreams.

INNER EXPLORATION

World View

- Write a statement that your father (or any other important care-taker) might have made that tells how the world really is. This may have been a motto for how to survive or be successful, such as "It's not what you know but who you know that counts in this world."

- Have you accepted this perspective as true for you? In what ways?

- Perhaps you have rebelled actively against a belief held by an important teacher from your childhood. If so, what view have you been reacting against, and how has your reaction affected you?

- Are your dreams showing characters with one particular stance, belief system or world view? For example, in your dreams do you continuously deal with, run from, or argue with bossy, dominating or controlling characters who perpetuate a certain belief?

- Does dream ego try to sell one particular perspective to others in your dreams?

Dreams of Forgetting or Losing

- Are you aware of dreams about forgetting something important? These can be warnings that, when understood, can help to identify an important part of life or self that is in danger. If you have such a dream or series, you probably will experience a great deal of relief by working through the symbols and metaphors to discover and then recover what is in danger.

CHAPTER ELEVEN

Work Strand

When we reach a certain level of recovery, we have to look at the way we do our work and see if the way we do our work threatens our sobriety.

Anne Wilson Schaef,
Beyond Therapy, Beyond Science

Only recently recognized as an addiction, workaholism still receives a great deal of support in our society. The phrase *I'm working* has a certain unassailable air of goodness and duty to it. The truth is, we are often working to avoid ourselves, our spouses, our feelings.

Julia Cameron,
The Artist's Way

T he first Victor dream of 1990 continued the healing theme begun in 1989. It shifts from the personal world view which had exacerbated my physical illnesses to illustrate an addictive syndrome common to a segment of our culture: compulsive work habits or "workaholism."

Victor Escapes Again   APRIL 13, 1990

I'm visiting an exciting school in Europe run by an insanely hyperactive principal. He runs from job to job in a manic fashion. Watching him, I feel anxious and somehow shameful. It seems there is a need for secrecy here.

I have drawn a large picture of the class doing gymnastic exercises. Everyone is admiring this drawing.

Six or seven of the nice guys from my high school class are attending this school. I see Vic walking around in the halls during class time and say, "Hey, Vic! I see you're still playing hooky!" I know that he wants to escape from the system, the structure created by this maniacal principal.

I was overtaken by a fit of laughing and coughing as I wrote the following in my journal: "I'm in an old world place *(Europe)* controlled by a compulsive, workaholic principle. I must really focus on the many ways in which I am turning myself *inside out* and *performing* in a very controlled fashion *(the gymnastics drawing)*. I need to see that *Vic has escaped* from this demanding scene because that is what *I* must do!"

I wrote that dream from what felt like my deathbed. A severe case of the flu, which had developed into pneumonia, had consumed my first vacation in two years. Until my body collapsed and grounded me, I had not realized that I had been caught in the pattern revealed in the dream. For two years preceding this dream I had worked non-stop, including weekend appointments and seminars. *Shame* and the need for *secrecy* mentioned in the dream arose because my behavior was opposite to the *principles* I had been learning and was therefore teaching. Most of my clients and students heard me speak of the value of daily moderation and balance to allow for reflective time. Without an opportunity to consider our lives, we have very little chance to exercise conscious choice. Though I was embracing this concept I had not been living it. The dream allowed me to experience the feelings my conscious self ignored.

It is significant that there is only masculine energy in this dream school. Unrecognized while I was awake, that powerful, focused, determined energy had consumed my work life. The boys in the dream school are *nice*, as productivity is *nice/good*, but it is not balanced by the feminine. This sense of *goodness* in work, even insanely unbalanced productivity, is greatly rewarded in our culture. The feminine relational, feeling, sacred elements can be lost easily.

Feeling both the excitement and anxiety in the dream reminded me of my former years of addicted behavior. A powerful adrenalin response occurs whether one is getting high from a substance or from an activity. It feels like aliveness—but, for me, it eventually results in physical and mental burnout. That adrenalin busy-ness also destroys the soul's need for time and attention to *process* life, not just whiz through it unexamined.

Playing Hooky Series (1982–1986)

Studying this particular dream reminded me of an entire branch of the Victor dream series which had clarified my inner desire to quit teaching, to escape from the system. The Playing Hooky Series lasted for more than four years and ended when I began half-time teaching to pursue professional dreamwork. In the beginning, the series showed me being reluctant to return to my class of students at the end of recesses. In dream after dream, I wanted to remain in the staff room discussing dreams with others while doing my own journal work. My reluctance evolved into rebellion as I instructed my dream aide to take the class without me. In the final dreams of this series, free of guilt or anxiety, I did not return to the classroom at all because I knew the children could care for themselves with the help of parent volunteers.

In high school Vic was the only person I knew who played hooky consistently. It seemed to me that he came to class or not, as he pleased. I was in awe of that kind of freedom/rebellion which I couldn't fathom for myself. In the *Victor Escapes Again* dream, he again played the quiet rebel, in this case a shadow character, showing me the destructive pattern I had established by working six days a week in my new dream career.

I devoted much attention to *Victor Escapes Again* because my work habits were so important to my overall health. I realized that it was easy to devote too much of my time to my new full-time career because the work itself was food for my soul. It was the only work I had ever done that energized me. In addition, I received a great deal of positive feedback which was repairing my old wounded sense of self. Nevertheless, too much of any good thing eventually turns into its opposite, as this dream and my rebelling body persistently demonstrated.

Contemplating the message of this dream, I understood that the strength of the spider's web was attributable to my mindset about work. I realized that my psyche was focusing continuously on this process. The *playing hooky* dreams had urged me to escape from a career which I had once loved but had now outgrown and was hanging on to out of fear and financial insecurity.

The Playing Hooky Series was prominent in my mind for several days. I wrote about and, for the first time, consciously recognized how really stuck I had been in the latter years of my former teaching career. After my illness (and my vacation!) ended, I returned to my private practice, continuing to wonder about the power and consequences of work habits. Then, as often happens to bring me more fully into consciousness about a significant issue, three experiences synchronistically occurred within one week to provide the clarity for which I was searching.

One Monday afternoon a seven-year-old client and I were sitting at my kitchen counter pounding clay into images from our dreams. My hands were too dirty and occupied to turn down the volume of the telephone answering machine as it recorded a message from an adult client. The seven-year-old asked, "Who that was on the phone?" After I answered, the boy asked if I played clay with "the phone man." "No," I answered, "but we do play with his dreams in other ways."

After a silence, the boy piped in with, "How do you make your living?"

"Pretty much doing what you and I do, only with lots of people of all ages," I responded.

"But you love playing with me, don't you?" he pursued, the question furrowing his face.

"I sure do, and I love working with other clients, too."

He frowned more deeply, showing his determination to understand a confounding notion. *"But what do you do to pay your bills at the end of the month?"* he shouted in frustration.

Trying again, I elaborated on the types of clients I served and the types of work we did.

"No! No!," he shouted, banging the counter. **"What do you do that you hate in order to pay your bills?"**

After recovering from the shock of this question, I acknowledged that all too often people earn money in ways they do not enjoy. I assured him that this was not a rule that he had to follow. The boy reported that his parents had told him that happiness comes from families, and these need lots of money. The only value of work is the money it produces to care for the families.

On Thursday of that same week a ten-year-old girl client and I were talking about her dream, which dealt with how much she hated school. Seemingly out of nowhere she asked how I earned my living. A shorter version of the conversation from Monday replayed, with this poignant ending: "Wow," she said, "I thought everyone was *supposed to* hate work the way kids hate school."

And finally, a friend reported a conversation she had with her adult son. The son asked how I was succeeding in my new career. His mom reported that everything looked great and that I was planning a work trip to Europe for the next summer. "Imagine that," the son said. "Someone can actually do what they love and survive."

I'm now convinced that my own similar beliefs about work created a great deal of the power that enabled the spider's web to ensnare the Eagle. The belief that work must be sacrifice kept me from pursuing full-time dreamwork for several years. Marsha Sinetar's book, *Do What You Love and the Money Will Follow*, examines in profound depth this cultural myth of suffering and work. Joseph Campbell, the grand teacher I met at Esalen who encouraged me to follow my dreams, taught the other side of this belief. He said that to follow one's bliss, what one truly loves, activates universal forces which then support the courageous decisions necessary to separate us from our security mania and move us into a life more fully lived.

Specifically appropriate to my personal journey is this passage about a young boy expressing fears about doing what he loves from Paulo Coelho's charming book *The Alchemist*:

> "My heart is afraid that it will have to suffer," the boy told the alchemist one night as they looked up at the moonless sky.
> "Tell your heart that the fear of suffering is worse than the suffering itself. And that no heart has ever suffered when it goes in search of its dreams."

That sentiment was proving to be a personal truth for me *as long as* I remained very conscious of the explicit guidance and warnings from my dreams.

Although much healing already had occurred, the following dream presents fresh fears of losing consciousness around the work process. The dream occurred in response to the creation of Dream Dance Company, a small business I developed with two other women to publish audiocassettes teaching the dream process with excerpts from my weekly radio show. The expanded public exposure and demands of our little company threatened *to get away from me* until this dream .

Vic and the Runaway Computer
OCTOBER 5, 1990

Vic and I are finally together. I'm intently telling him that we must return to our home town. We create a computer in a suitcase to help us.

At one point the machine gets away from us and rolls down a hill. Vic runs to retrieve it. When he returns he has become George Pettit and is petulant, bitchy, whiny and nasty. He says he won't do anything anymore. I'm very upset and disappointed that Vic has been replaced by George.

The scene shifts. Vic and I are talking to Jane Kelly. I comment that her mother was the only mom I knew in high school who felt to me like a real mother. "Please remember to give her my love," I say.

The sought-after masculine way of being in the world (Vic)—relaxed, self-contained, quietly rebellious, casual—transforms into a whiny, no-can-do, recalcitrant, bitchy energy when my way of working *(computer)* in the suitcase *(old baggage)* gets away from me. At one level that could certainly refer to workaholism.

The resolution to that unconscious kind of takeover lies in the second scene. (These little tag-on endings of dreams often seem like throw-aways but are usually important to the overall issue presented by the dream.) Jane, a high school friend, was blessed with a mom who was the epitome of the Earth Mother. I had not thought of her for at least twenty years, but this dream enlivened the powerfully accepting, nurturing, humorous energy she presented to all of Jane's friends. I remember Jane inviting me to her house for lunch the day after one of my mother's suicide attempts. Mrs. Kelly had set the table with flowers, candles, and fine china. "I thought this might help," she said. And it surely did.

Following the *when/then* of this dream, *when* the work process gets away—exchanging helpful masculine energy for whiny, wimpy, inadequacy—*then* I must remember the truly sensitive and supportive mother energy. Ah ha! As long as I remember that *nurturing* force, the work process *does not* get away from me. I then can make decisions, say yes or no, based on what is truly best for all parts of me, physically, emotionally, and spiritually. Because of its protective nature, this mothering energy automatically shuts down the uncontrolled *doer* which leads to burnout.

Thinking about this dream led me to recall my mother's work process. She often became an obsessed maniac, forcing herself to work until early hours of the morning despite rage and crying attacks when inevitable problems occurred with her project. She was a remarkably talented and tenacious woman, but unbalanced work habits were intricately entwined with a victim/martyr self-image. Arriving at this memory showed me why Vic and I had to go back to our home town in this dream. Spending imaginal time there showed me how much I had altered the destructive processes modeled by my mother and reminded me that I had spent years developing inner nurturing parental forces, represented by Jane's mom. I felt safe enough with these realizations to move on, saying *yes* to professional expansion without being blocked by a whiny and overwhelmed inner masculine/doer.

Often a dream provides the opportunity to see the growth and progress we have made. Examining a dream that shows me the resolution of a formerly debilitating process allows me to proceed with renewed hope and courage. Each such realization led me to acknowledge that another strand of the web had been severed.

INNER EXPLORATION
Work Tapes

- Our beliefs whirl around on our internal tapes, driving us without our personal awareness. Can you hear your internalized beliefs about work and working? You may have identified some of these tapes while considering your parents' world view in Chapter Ten.

- Often people discard dreams which center on the workplace, saying that they are only thinking about what happened the day before. Beware of that rationalization.

  Write and work with your *work* dreams. Look for repeating feelings and happenings within the dreams.

  Look for changes from dream to dream. What do you notice?

- Look for dream characters who react very differently from the way you usually do in work situations. How might these *shadow* characters be of value to you?

Tag Ends

- Choose five dreams from your journal. Look for the *tag-ends*, the strange little additions at the end of dreams that seem to be disconnected from the rest of the dream.

  Can you identify the metaphor contained within the snippet? Might that present a resolution to an issue presented in the rest of the dream?

  Could the *add-on* be a suggestion for the future, somewhat like a foreshadowing in a novel?

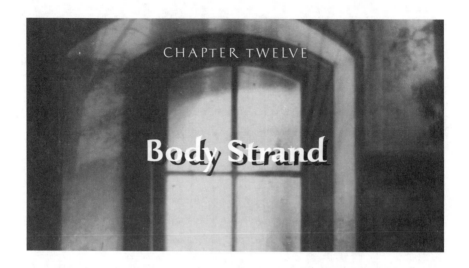

CHAPTER TWELVE

Body Strand

If we were to examine our diseases poetically, we might find a
wealth of imagery that could speak to the way we live our lives.
Following up on that imagery, we could attune our lives and allow
ourselves *to be corrected* by the disease. *[emphasis added]*

Thomas Moore, *Care of the Soul*

Extended physical illness can become another opening. We often
hear about radical changes brought about by insights that come
when a person is forced to inactivity and is given an opportunity to
turn inward and contemplate what is overlooked most of the time.
It may begin the question, What is the meaning of this illness?
Or, better still, What can I learn from this illness?

June Singer, *Seeing Through the Visible World*

dentifying and changing my compulsive work patterns was a demanding process. Even more difficult was dealing with a plethora of physical complaints that had plagued me for years. Chronic, extensive food allergies, candidiasis, hypoglycemia, consistent dizziness, headaches, horrific skin eruptions, and incessant exhaustion had frightfully diminished my participation in normal life experiences. For undetected reasons my immune system was severely compromised. Doctors could not understand the tenacity of these various complaints which had not been alleviated by fourteen years of an extremely limited and painfully boring diet, controlled activity, and environment. Finally, a doctor found a type of intestinal parasite for which there was no known treatment. I was told that hosting this nasty little critter sapped all my physical resources, leaving nothing to heal the other complications. From the perspective of the traditional medical model, I felt doomed to live the half-life of a Chronic Fatigue Syndrome patient forever.

However, my understanding of the healing potential of the human mind would not allow me to succumb to a belief in the irreversible continuation of these problems. My study of the mind/body connection revealed the power of attitude in the course of healing. I was beginning to question whether it was my body or my soul that was "sick." I was resonating with ideas like this one from Frances Vaughan in her book, *Shadows of the Sacred* :

> Since ancient times healing practices have been intimately connected with the soul. In our secular society, however, when people feel threatened by the shadow of illness, they usually turn to medicine in search of healing for both body and mind. In my experience, the soul is not responsive to conventional medical interventions. It is not a mechanism to be fixed or a biological organism that responds readily to biochemical alterations. From the point of view of the soul, a person may ask about the meaning of illness or discover spiritual healing in the face of death.

Thus, I was willing to search for healing outside of mainstream medicine.

My 1989 dream about helping Victor recover from alcohol (Chapter Ten) led me to see that I was, in a meaningful way, psychologically addicted to my illness. Thereafter, I began attending lectures and workshops about healing the physical body by identifying beliefs that either created or exacerbated chronic illness. I was devoted to a spiritual program which supported all of these beliefs and stretched beyond even those paradigms.

I was fascinated by ideas such as this one presented by Thomas Moore in *Care of the Soul:* "The human body is an immense source of imagination, a field on which imagination plays wantonly. The body is the soul presented in its richest and most expressive form. In the body, we see the soul articulated in gesture, dress, movement, shape, physiognomy, temperature, *skin eruptions,* tics, *diseases in countless expressive form.*" [emphasis added]. I was determined to discover what my soul was articulating. I was convinced that my dreams were the voice of my soul and that the healing of my body would manifest through the images and insight given by my dreams.

As my consciousness in this area grew I found many talented and loving alternative healing practitioners. Some of them helped me plow through layers of buried pain in hopes of bringing relief for my body. Others helped me identify the parts of myself that valued illness. I learned to admit to a "Camille" aspect of myself which enjoyed the special attention that illness brought, but was absolutely *no* fun to hang out with for long. I certainly couldn't take "Camille" to Europe, a voyage which became my goal in 1990. I was determined to be free of all vestiges of illness by the summer of 1991 so that I could work and visit friends in Germany and Austria.

To that end, I began treatment with a wonderful herbalist, laughingly telling him he had a year to strengthen my body enough to allow me to eat German bread and drink German beer. A dream the night after our first session predicted this possibility. In the dream I joyfully show the herbalist my new "used" car. We look under the hood and see a spotlessly clean engine shining like a huge jewel!

The following dream also provided a great deal of delight and hope. At the time I was dealing with termites in the wooden beams of my adobe house. I joked that finding an alternative to toxic house-tenting was a metaphor for ridding my body of its internal parasites through alternative methods. An electro-gun zapped the termites while my dreamer treated the parasites with the following gem.

From Termites to Transformation: Emergence   JULY 12, 1990

I'm in a shop filling out the papers to have my termite problem treated. As I write my elbow hits a cocoon, allowing a beautiful white caterpillar/kitten creature to emerge. I'm amazed because I thought the cocoon was dead. The termite man and I are both delighted that, in this place of riddance, such a lovely thing exists. We each hold the kitten-sized creature tenderly in our arms, loving it dearly.

Returning our attention to the paper work, I question the need for an emergency number for this procedure. The man insists, and I give him Vic and his wife's phone number.

There are two more cocoons on my left and another furry creature emerges. This one is black, large and elegant, and as precious as the white one. I'm enchanted.

One more cocoon exists. Is something in it, I wonder?

My journal records the following: "This is the dream of a woman who is preparing to rid herself of internally destructive, unseen forces (*termites;* that which consumes or destroys structures, in this case, her body). In doing so, what she thought was dead emerges, very much alive, adorable, embraceable, and balanced (white and black) or known and still unconscious. The amazing process of transformation is not yet complete as one more cocoon remains."

I called two friends to share this dream and celebrate its meaning. As I read the dream to them, I felt both joy and a definite edge of fear. The possibility of *wellness* threatened the structure of my life, since I had for so long adjusted to the demands and "benefits" of illness. Could I actually make the transitions necessary for a fully functioning life? If so, could I be safe from the ravages of addiction that preceded the illnesses? Did I *really* want to *emerge* from the protective cocoon provided by fifteen years of illness? What dangers might I experience if I could no longer hide behind the excuse of illness? All of these surprising feelings substantiated the *addiction to illness* theme from the dream seven months before *(Helping Victor Recover from Booze*, Chapter Ten).

Using the image of the cocoon I was able to see my years of illness in a different light. My illnesses had definitely encased and surrounded me. What if they had been providing protection for the incubation of new elements of self /soul now apparently ready to become activated? That question produced a strong body hit. As my heart sped up, my skin began to tingle. My emotions registered both excitement and fear. If that were true, what was going to emerge and could I handle whatever it was?

Seeing, feeling, and holding the lovable and wondrous *caterpillar/kitten* reduced my resistance to what could emerge. If the image had been a caterpillar/python or caterpillar/machine, my healing process undoubtedly would have been hampered. But these wondrous creatures, adored by both dream ego and the exterminator, soothed my scared, resistant self, as did the metaphor entwined within the *emergency number*. The "ah ha" occurred when a friend pointed out the connection between the *emergence* of the creatures from the cocoon and the emergency number. In case of *emergence*, call the force which has been so long valued and sought! Bingo! Again Victor takes the role of extracting the Eagle energy, in this case entrapped by the strand of physical illness.

The next dream shows the level of integration necessary for the mind/body work to be effective. It brought as much hope as the *Termites to Transformation* dream.

Esalen Lecture
(Psychosomatic Illness)   OCTOBER 19, 1990

I'm at Esalen and see Vic and his wife. I'm excited to see them but do not approach them.

Then I am talking to a group there as the Bientos listen. I can't tell if I'm lecturing as an "expert" or simply sharing personal experience, but I say clearly, "Much chronic physical illness is psychosomatic. Once the mind is healed the body heals."

Over the years of working with my dreams I've noticed that an *internal acceptance* has occurred when dream ego lectures within a dream. This deep, inner self-teaching is necessary for a major shift in attitude or behavior. In this dream I am admitting to the psychological component of my illnesses. I seem to be reassuring myself that pursuing alternative healing processes and looking for the *psychosomatic* aspects to my illness is the right thing to do.

To be at Esalen is to be in a place where much healing has occurred, where outdated collective beliefs are replaced by emerging paradigms, and where Joseph Campbell told me to pursue the Eagle Dream. It makes sense that I would take myself back to that psychic environment to reinforce something as important as self-healing.

This dream brought a deeper, more fearless commitment to the healing path I had chosen nearly a year before. Most people struggling to decide which healing protocol to follow probably would agree that the stress of doubt diminishes one's ability to heal. The Esalen dream erased my last concerns about that doubt, replacing conflict with enormous relief.

The next dream puts another spin on illness.

"Crazy" Vic in Nepal   JANUARY 19, 1991

I'm with a group of people in Nepal. Victor Biento is with us. He is clearly "crazy" though this is experienced by looking at him, not by his behavior. There is a wild, unnatural look about him. I think this is the look of a "crazy shaman" like the holy men in Nepal. I'm not frightened but just curious as I study him sitting at a bar.

When I awoke, I knew it was *right* that Victor was crazy. I thought about a discussion my dream-training group had with James Hillman about honoring the "insane" within us, as it is not the compliant, tethered energy to which we usually pledge our allegiance. I thought how "crazy" I was to quit the security of public school teaching to follow the dream. I vividly recalled the intense feeling of insanity attached to the Eagle Dream, without which I would not have pursued that particular dream. I doubt I would be physically alive if that dream had not motivated the transformation of my life. Clearly, in these cases, *insanity* worked.

Several of my friends have spent time in Nepal. Hearing about their experiences, I have come to think of Nepal as a spiritual center. Thus, for me, to be in Nepal is to be in a place of higher consciousness. What happens here, metaphorically, is ruled not by the ego but by the transpersonal self.

I had been impressed by friends' reports of seeing crazy-looking shamans in Nepal and South America. These healers are respected for their "divine insanity." I recalled writings about people identified as shamans or healers in other cultures. Often an ordinary individual has a near-death experience, a life-threatening illness, or a mental breakdown of some kind. Many consider this not a *breakdown* but a *break through*. Surviving the traumatic life-altering experience seems to connect the once-common person to different ways of seeing and knowing which transform her/him into a valuable healer.

Seeing Vic—the sought-after energy—in this light and in a *bar* (a place of the spirits) turned my head in yet another direction. It allowed a different perspective of my chronic physical problems. What if all this misery were serving a *valuable* purpose? What if it had provided a *cocoon* for new growth (former dream) and, metaphorically, created *shamanic* qualities and a *divinely insane* way of perceiving reality which could be helpful to my work with people? Without question, all the learning I had acquired in my healing journey had deeply impacted the ways in which I worked with clients.

Seeing possible value and meaning in the illness—beyond the wake-up call from my abused body and soul—allowed me to be more accepting of the process of illness. Until these last two dreams, I had been angry and resentful about the lost years that illness had taken from me. No emotion keeps me attached to a person or an issue more than constant anger. In order to move on, I needed to release the anger by seeing myself not as a *victim* but as a *recipient* of growth.

The human process always has its swings of the pendulum. Thus, after six months of improved health which I attributed to alternative healing procedures, I received the following dream, which revealed a threat to my continued recovery.

The Threat to Recovery   FEBRUARY 13, 1991

We are all in danger from a murderer who is responsible for Vic's disappearance. I am dispatched to find Vic but he returns on his own, drunk. It is now my job to help him recover if I can.

The next morning I make contact with Vic. Clearly, I must woo and win him over to the recovery process or the murderer will get him, too. Vic warms up to me as we talk and agrees to cooperate with the plan for recovery. We will begin after the Fourth of July.

It's July 5th. I'm working with Vic's mother, who needs to be educated if Vic is to be safe. I'm giving her an illustration of effective healthy confrontation skills to help her stand up to her husband. This is necessary to protect the family.

When Mr. Biento joins us, she explains about Vic and the recovery program. We need Mr. Biento to participate in the healing. He tells me that, frankly, he thinks the program is a crock. It is little more than the blind leading the blind.

I say that I understand, and even agree in part, but that, at this time, it is the best process for addicts. It is imperative that I win over this man for the safety of the whole family. I need his agreement to work with Vic. Mr. Biento is hearing me and I am hopeful.

In the wily way of illness, I had suffered a fairly severe relapse a week before this dream, reactivating my feelings of hopelessness about recovery. This had caused my vital, extricating "Vic energy" to disappear altogether. I certainly experienced the recurrence of old symptoms as a *murderer* of joy and the healthy life for which I so desperately yearned. My conscious self (dream ego) had work to do to *recover* what I had lost.

This setback caused me to doubt the non-conventional healing approaches I was using. The challenging energy in my psyche was the father, the masculine, which judged the healing process I wanted to use as unacceptable, as not clearly seen (*blind leading the blind*). Linking the healing process to *recovery*, I had suffered a *slip*—a recovery term for a relapse into former unhealthy thinking or behaving. All of my former beliefs about hopelessness and futility resurfaced. In addition, my logical masculine side clearly felt the alternative choices I was pursuing were unwise. But it was apparently willing to learn.

In the *Taming the Rebel/Teaching the Rebel* dream (Chapter Five), Victor knew about the Tories, who I identified as the "repressors" of my Irish ancestors. This dream says that freedom from that force must be celebrated (*Fourth of July*) before the recovery process can begin. Since the Eagle Dream I had been confronting repressive inner psychic forces of all kinds. In the larger context the repressors are the beliefs and forces holding the eagle in the web. In this dream I saw that repressive force as the logical, intellectual component in my psyche (the masculine, the father) which wanted to repress my enthusiasm for psycho/spiritual healing. The dream says the *mother* (the intuitive, feeling component) must *be educated*, so that she has the strength to *confront the husband*. This notion highlighted a dynamic of conflict between the masculine (*logical*) and the feminine (*spiritual*) processes discussed in Chapter Eight.

By saying that a murderer threatened *Victor*, this dream allowed me to see the seriousness of my recent slip. Identifying that the logical element (the masculine, father) was the obstacle to healing allowed me to focus upon my reservations and resolve them. I did this using the lecturing model from the former dream. I imagined myself at Esalen, speaking to a large and receptive group about all I had learned about non-traditional recovery. I wrote letters to the doubting dream father delineating all the growth and healing I had experienced thus far. During daily walks I focused on my faith in this ephemeral process. After several days I was able to return to my unknown, untried path (*blind leading the blind*) with renewed faith and conviction. Extricated from the *murderous forces* of doubt and distrust, my physical body continued to improve.

I am not suggesting that I abandoned the importance of the rational mind and its wondrous abilities. Doing so would be the same kind of *either/or* repression represented by the Tories in Chapter Five. A fully functioning individual uses all the abilities and possibilities available. And so, after ten unsuccessful years working within the traditional medical model, I had admitted to myself that the continuation of my physical ailments was psycho-spiritual in origin. The point of this dream signifies the importance of healing the *psyche* as well as the *soma*, which meant allegiance to my psycho/spiritual approach regardless of the inner conflict it created.

I did go to Europe in 1991, able to eat and drink whatever I wanted for the first time in sixteen years. I hiked, shopped, and partied with no loss of energy despite jet lag and a work schedule. The friends I visited had known me throughout my illnesses and were as amazed and delighted as I that my *engine* was clean, my *termites* were gone, and new, precious life forms were emerging. A higher *insane* spiritual perspective had enabled most of the healing I had sought for so long. Only one severe ailment remained. The next chapter, on self-esteem, focuses on that problem.

INNER EXPLORATION
Merged Symbols

• Blended images provide us with a very creative opportunity and challenge. A combination of symbols paints a very specific picture that asks to be seen, to be felt. Here is one way to play with these magical combinations.

First define each of the separate parts. Then blend the two parts together and see what is created.

Let's work with a *motorcycle-sailboat*, an example from one of my clients.

> "A motorcycle is a powerful, noisy, usually individual way of moving which demands personal balance. Motorcycles scare me but I sort of admire people who ride them. I think they are kind of rebellious.
> A boat is the way to get around on the water. It keeps you afloat. It goes with the flow and rides the waves. I think of water as emotions, so a boat may be a way of staying on top of or in control of my feelings. Therefore I need a powerful, slightly rebellious, balanced way of staying in control of my feelings."

• After working with the images, allow them to bridge or connect to the awake world, if that seems appropriate. Here is the bridge created for the above dreamer:

"My mother was always awash with feelings. She was rarely able to cope with her emotions and took to her bed with migraines. I need to rebel against that defense because I can fall into this, too. I need to remember the personal power that comes from being balanced in situations rather than just blowing in the wind, like a sailboat. I need to be at the helm, making quick decisions like the cyclist must make."

CHAPTER THIRTEEN

Self-Esteem

The universal psychological wound of Western culture is unworthiness, the soul sickness of low self-esteem that underlies psychological and religious pessimism. Most people are fiercely self-critical, having internalized the shaming voices of their parental figures. They secretly believe that whatever they do is not good enough, that other people would not like them if they really knew them, that they are selfish, bad or simply not as competent as others.

Joan Borysenko, *Fire in the Soul*

If you continue to replay the same negative thoughts and feelings that have burdened you for many years, you will continue to have the same *physiology*. [*emphasis added*]

Deepak Chopra, *Perfect Weight*

Perhaps, at some level, all inner work deals with, redefines, and heals our sense of self. When I truly engage with a dream, I usually learn something previously unknown about myself. I may be confronted by feelings, beliefs, or behaviors I have denied or simply never recognized. I may view an unknown facet of myself in relationship with others—intimately, socially, or professionally. The dream may expose an inner process, a way in which I am interacting (inner-acting) with various parts of myself. Now and then, I'm privileged to catch a glimpse of my transpersonal self, that spiritual being beyond my ego and personality, which escapes the bounds of the material world and knows no limits. And each of these dream experiences shifts the way I understand and esteem myself, which in turn, alters the ways I relate to others.

Getting below the surface of our everyday facades and defenses is one of the greatest, albeit most uncomfortable, gifts of the dream. Several dreams already presented certainly tapped into my painful sense of inadequacy during my high school years, the years when I knew Victor. The following dream, one of my *least* favorite, explores this issue as it related to my chronic illness and professional work.

Crooked, Covered-Up Vic in Kitchen
MAY 13, 1991

I'm with a group of high school kids. We're in a tiny kitchen containing a gas stove. A very ugly Vic Biento is present. His face is somehow crooked, hideously broken out, and poorly covered with makeup. Still, I want his attention and I want to be part of the group. I know they don't want me there but I won't leave.

All are pitching in to cook a meal. I'm painfully aware of being ignored by everybody. I need to do something so I will at least seem busy. I join Victor and put a pot on to cook. I'm intrigued by the instant heat from the gas stove. I would like to cook something on all four burners.

I notice a big clunky bracelet on my right arm. It's probably not the fashionable thing to wear. Maybe this is why I'm being rejected.

In my journal I wrote, "I hate this dream and don't want to work it." I was fully aware that examining the crooked, broken out, ugly face of dream Victor was deeply distasteful, for he mirrored what I could not bear to see in myself.

I left the dream but it did not leave me. Eventually, I submitted to its power and worked it several times with different people. At the literal level, each painful session activated unpleasant memories of my earlier life and of feeling excluded in high school. Significantly, the most traumatic element of my chronic illness *(facial sores)* is also seen in this piece.

In order to understand the time in my past to which the dream returned me, the following background is needed. I went to a small and unusual school in a very beautiful, wealthy, exclusive area. I loved my time there as intensely as I hated it. It seemed to me then that nearly all of my classmates were rich kids with highly respectable professional parents: doctors, lawyers, judges, successful merchants. I definitely did not qualify for what I considered that elite club, and felt excluded from the day of my entrance in elementary school. During these fragile years of severe comparison I always saw myself on the bottom of social strata. I felt as if I were an unacceptable alien in a beautiful, bountiful but inhospitable land.

During all my teen years I worried obsessively about caring for my mother. This anxiety created insomnia by night and "daydreaming" in class. Thus, my scholastic performance was less than sterling. In short, I usually felt ugly, poor, stupid, and ashamed of my parents, myself, and our lifestyle.

Normal teenage acne caused me enormous shame. Thirty years later a similar condition was one of the symptoms of my chronic adult illness. For many years I suffered from minor but upsetting facial outbreaks which were attributed to candida. Then, while taking a new prescription to combat this ailment, I awoke one morning to find my pillow covered with pus and blood. I could feel something oozing from my chin, leapt from bed to mirror to find a raw, bloody chin and a disfiguring ailment which plagued me for four more years.

Most of the time, several layers of facial *makeup* and powder would allow me to work and feel somewhat comfortable in public. But there were many episodes when I would not leave the house nor see clients because seepage from the open wounds would break through my makeup, leaving bloody patches on my face. I felt like the Elephant Woman and despaired of ever being able to present myself without layers of masking.

Many dreams, including the *Covered-Up Vic* dream, revealed a great deal about the psychological component of my illness. I read many books describing illness as metaphor, which led me to suspect that I was unable to *face* the world without intricately applied and maintained *cover-up*. This was very frustrating to the part of me yearning to be free of *cover-ups* like alcohol, food, and unhealthy compliance with others' wishes. I wanted to be bare, open, honest (not *crooked*), and accepted for my authentic self (not *rejected*). Instead, I often felt the need to be heavily defended (*armed*, as in the bracelet in the dream), causing others to *reject* me. Instead of *cooking on all four burners* I barely had a pilot light. Though I was functioning professionally and socially, I felt as if I were constantly dragging myself through lakes of mud to accomplish any task.

At a concrete level, at the time of the above dream I was considering quitting my public radio talk show devoted to teaching the process of the dream. I was exhausted after each weekly program and felt unable to *face* it any more. While on air, I was aware of *hiding* my own beliefs and process about the dream behind the quotes and work of others in the field. As I studied Vic's face in the dream I saw my own crookedness, my lack of honesty in my radio work. I suspected the symbol had more depth but couldn't reach it at the time.

The one decision I was able to make as a result of this dream was to *remove my makeup* and present myself openly on the show. I began to share views which differed from other dream teachers but which my personal and professional experience verified. As I became bolder each week, the show drew larger audiences and more kudos. Stepping out in this way often gave me the sensation of manifesting the quiet rebel energy of Victor Biento. After one particularly feisty show a listener called to say he liked the way I was soaring! Naturally, the eagle came to mind.

After the *Covered-Up Vic* dream I decided to attend both professional and social activities whether my face was oozing or not. When the episodes were particularly gruesome and the oozing couldn't be covered, I was able to meet clients with no makeup at all. I discovered that in all cases people respected my work and accepted me, disfigured face or not. I have no doubt that all of those experiences helped to heal the very roots of this syndrome, which many years later finally was diagnosed as a chronic staph infection.

The healing of a shattered sense of self is a complex, multi-faceted procedure. The acceptance of friends, clients, and listening audience allowed me to esteem myself differently. Each experience of being accepted for my authentic self was valuable, but nothing in the awake world was more impactful than the following dream featuring Victor Biento. It occurred three weeks after *Crooked, Covered-Up Victor*, and felt like a sequel.

Victor's Healing Embrace   MAY 29, 1991

I've been out running errands and having lunch with friends. I'm anxious to get home and hide. My face is horribly broken out again and I feel ashamed. I just want to remove my makeup and be alone.

> *On the way to the bathroom I am amazed to see Victor Biento sitting on the couch. My God, what is he doing here? I'm thrilled to see him but I must not allow him to see me because I look so terrible. I dash into the bathroom, quietly shut the door and begin to cry in sorrow and shame.*
>
> *Almost immediately the door is gently pushed open and Vic forces his way in. He takes me in his arms and holds me, rocking tenderly, saying over and over, "It's ok, it's ok." I sob deeply and joyfully.*

Interpretation is unnecessary, but my *response* to the dream is vital to understanding the overall healing story presented in this book. My willingness to show my authentic, uncovered face in public in this dream was reinforced by the deep compassion and total acceptance of Victor, that energy so long sought and so highly valued. The unconditional acceptance I felt in this dream healed my heart, soul, and body at a depth which cannot be touched by medication, talk therapy, body work, Chinese medicine, or hypnosis. I was so impacted by this dream I could not share it for several weeks. The only other dream with so much power was the Eagle dream and surely, one leads inevitably to the other and to the writing of this book.

After that dream, when I became conscious of berating or rejecting myself, I would remind myself that Victor was able to accept me as I was. I could then relax in the luxury of previously unknown, unconditional self-acceptance.

Victor's Healing Embrace could appropriately have been presented in the former chapter on the Body Strand for it certainly figures in the healing of the chronic illnesses. It feels a better fit here because I'm now convinced that as I grew to esteem my self and trust the world, my physical body changed and healed.

How tidy it would be to end this chapter here. But, alas, human development is rarely so orderly. So, on to the next dream, reflecting self-esteem issues on a slightly different front.

Unworthy Vic   APRIL 6, 1993

Mother and I are on a trip to the town where Vic lives. We have come to talk to Vic about the book. Vic's wife is worried that he will not want to cooperate with the publication because he thinks of himself as not laudable or worthy of attention. He thinks he was an awful person in high school. His wife fears he will not be able to see beyond that.

I like the model of seeing human development as a spiral, reaching into ever higher levels of consciousness but always hitting the same life issues as we traverse the ellipse. Thus I expect to always deal with a "not good enough" sense of self each time I reach another level of accomplishment. So it was with this dream, which occurred shortly after I realized that this book project had a real chance of being published. I had suffered one attack of severe anxiety and self-doubt when my first audiocasette was published and distributed in 1991. Here I was again, on another rung of the spiral, dealing with the same sense of inadequacy.

I was grateful for this dream's warning about resistance. Without that warning this book project might have been seriously jeopardized. Because of the dream I listened clearly to my inner voices and countered each fear that arose from the unhealed self.

In addition to my awake work, dream help arrived about six months later. The following dream illustrates a quote from Jeremy Taylor about the value of working with the symbolic elements of physical illness: "…interior explorations

that lead to increased self-awareness and self-understanding, and to more accepting, forgiving, and consciously creative self-concepts, can and regularly do have
a profound and positive effect on physical health and healing."

Gifts at the Reunion   NOVEMBER 18, 1993

*I'm excited to be at my high school reunion. I see Vic sitting at
a long table chatting with others. I'm looking forward to the
time we will get together for a long talk about the dream series.*

*I'm sitting in a scattered informal circle with the girls
from my class, my former friends, and others who never
accepted me. We're teasing and laughing intimately. I'm
surprised and delighted with the joy and comfort I feel here
for I have forgotten to put on my makeup!*

*Annie says she wants to buy me a blouse in appreciation
for all the public work I've done. I'm surprised and delighted
that she both knows and cares about my work.*

*Now we're all in the Phoenix Shop at Nepenthe's. It's
fun to be appreciated and to look for the gift with these
women who are now good friends.*

This dream speaks of a woman who is *reunited* and comfortable with that
which she formerly feared. This is the dream of a woman who is happy to be
authentic *(without makeup)*. This is a dream about a woman who feels accepted
and valued.

When the transformation from inner self-hatred and rejection finally
occurs, this dream woman is able to receive the *gifts* which come from *rebirth*
(the Phoenix, the symbol of transformation and rebirth). In my journal I
wrote, "This dream beautifully illustrates the inner sense of self-acceptance
which has taken so many years of healing work to manifest." The next sentence surprised me when it *appeared* on the page: "Most of the time I feel that

I can *face* anything and should never again need the staph infection to protect me from being open and exposed with others." My intuition was accurate, for I have not suffered a devastating staph outbreak since.

As we address and heal one element of our wounded psyche, another facet may come forward. Thus it is with the following dream, which focuses on a sense of inadequacy in another context.

Town Reunion and
Disreputable Vic   MAY 3, 1994

I'm at the "town" reunion. The old high school class has gathered to observe the lives of the kids who still live in town. We will also attend gatherings and parties. In a small food market, I see a clerk who reminds me of Vic Biento.

I ask a group of guys from my graduating class if the clerk is Vic. Though they affirm this I'm astonished because of his disreputable appearance. I approach him, extending my hand, "Are you Vic Biento?" He nods. "I was in your class," I report. "I just want to say hi."

Turning away from him I feel sad and surprised. Though he has a smart modern haircut, he looks and smells like a pathetic creature hooked on booze and cigarettes. His skin is sallow and pitted. He seems very shy and undeveloped. I wonder if reading the book will have any impact on him. Will it help him to know how valuable he has been to me all these years even though he seems not to value himself?

In this piece, the Vic energy is described as *disreputable, pathetic, addicted, shy, and undeveloped.* Checking the dictionary, I was distressed to find the following synonyms for disreputable: notorious, base, dishonorable. As I worked the dream with an associate I had difficulty owning any of those descriptors.

After so much work on accepting, nurturing, and esteeming myself, I no longer *felt* like the dream Victor looked.

The mystery was solved when my dream partner asked the significance of a *town reunion*. Ah ha! a *town reunion* is a gathering in the *larger collective!* In this dream it was a reunion in the collective place of my childhood. Indeed, in an expanded environment I could still identify myself as *shy and undeveloped*, still responding *addictively* (cigarettes and booze) to old feelings of inadequacy.

The dream says we are to observe the lives of our classmates who *never left town*. The part of me that still lives and works in the state of consciousness I experienced in high school continues to feel unacceptable in a larger collective environment!

I was attracted to the contrast between Vic's stylish, modern haircut and his otherwise disreputable appearance. It seems that despite cutting off the old beliefs, feelings, and sense of self *(hair)*, a need for healing is still evident. I saw this as meaning that the intellectual work *(hair)* had been done but the changes were not yet internalized. The neocortex was convinced but the reptilian brain remained unchanged. This is always the process of freeing oneself from the past. It usually happens in very specific stages.

Vic works in a place that provides nourishment to the collective *(market)*. I hope and believe that's what I do, but I clearly need to address this issue of self-esteem if I am to break out of the environment of my earlier days. This strand of the web encircling the eagle is thick, sticky, and very tough, but the second dream of that night helps to sever it. It is presented in the next chapter.

INNER EXPLORATION

Resistance

- It is valuable to watch our reactions to writing down or working with a dream. Jot down any intense responses you have to a dream, as that may figure into the material itself.

- Our resistance to a dream may be heard through many voices: *I don't have time. It's just about the movie I saw last night. I already know what the dream is saying. I don't need to work on this issue anymore. It's not important. I shouldn't have eaten pizza so close to bedtime.*

- If you are so resistant to a dream piece that you cannot write it down, at least write about your feelings. Gently express what you are aware of and invite the dream to come again in a less threatening fashion.

- Report your resistance to a health professional, if you are working with one, or to a trusted friend. Often our fears will be alleviated by simply talking about them.

- If your resistance comes from a feeling of fear, check to see whether you are looking at the dream too literally. Often, fears about a dream will be resolved when it is examined symbolically and metaphorically. To begin that process, objectify dream ego and synthesize the dream with a statement like: This is the dream of a person who _____ (shift to metaphor).

For example: A man was terrified by a dream scene in which his mother was chasing him with a knife. He objectified it this way: "This is the dream about a man who is being attacked by an energy which is supposed to be nurturing." This led him to see how he was beating on rather than accepting himself.

CHAPTER FOURTEEN

Amends

There is a further consequence of the credit one pays to the images of the soul. A new feeling of self-forgiveness and self-acceptance begins to spread and circulate.

James Hillman,
The Blue Fire

The purpose [of making amends] is to restore us to right relation-ships—with ourselves and with other people.

Melody Beattie,
Codependents' Guide to the Twelve Steps

After fifteen years of searching for relief from the tenacious physical symptoms that debilitated me I turned from soma to psyche. Hoping to utilize the power of the dream, I incubated (requested) a dream asking for specific guidance. In my dream journal I wrote, "What focus should my physical healing take next?" I was amazed when my dreamer pulled up the issue of making amends to a person I had betrayed thirty years before.

Vic and Paul: Amends and Connections   FEBRUARY 2, 1991

I'm looking at a class picture. I zoom into and focus on images of Vic and Paul as they each were years ago, Vic in high school and Paul in college. I'm very excited, hoping that the owner of the photograph might be able to tell me where Paul and Vic are. Then I could make amends to Paul and hang out with Vic.

After ten years of almost daily dreamwork I had become familiar with the relief that comes from admitting the truth about myself, both the terrible and the sublime. My years partnering dream work with a program of recovery allowed me to make contact with the dark, denied parts of myself and to make amends for the behaviors that sprang from them.

A dream from 1982 presented the need for such work. In the dream, I lived on a smoldering plateau which was always too hot to be physically comfortable. No matter the thickness of my boots, the heat from below the surface made me hop around, never able to settle down or relax. Several years later I was to realize that the heat rose from feelings of guilt and shame about the ways in which I was or had been harmful to others. I was able to identify these *character defects* by owning the less than desirable characters in my dreams. Jungians refer to this as *shadow* work. I think of it as lifesaving activity because of its importance to my overall healing.

As I faced each disgusting aspect of my shadow, pressure from below was released. In practical terms I experienced this by a slow but obvious cessation of the headaches that had plagued me for fifteen years. After an intense piece of shadow work, or a conversation during which I would release a secret I had, to that point, buried (in the smoldering underground) I would not need to medicate my headaches for several hours. This was momentous since I otherwise needed two aspirin every four hours just to function.

I found that admitting a piece of my shadow to another person brought the most relief. Releasing *the secret* was akin to popping a pimple or taking the top off a boiling pot. The more shadow aspects I owned the more comfortable I was. With each piece of shadow work the temperature of the smoldering plateau decreased. Thus I could appreciate the focus that psyche provided by the Vic and Paul dream. Here's the background needed for this dream.

Paul was a generous and sensitive young man, my first love in college. After dating for more than a year we were considering marriage when I met someone else. With no concern or compassion, I dismissed Paul by writing a pitiable "Dear John" letter, trying to make him responsible for the end of the relationship. Heaping guilt on someone else was the best way to deny my own. At age eighteen I had not learned how *to face* others directly and honestly, so I could not face Paul with the truth.

I have always deeply regretted this cold-blooded act which froze into guilt which for years felt like a cold, hard, ever-present vise in the pit of my solar plexus. It strangled energy and held joy hostage. To successfully deny its presence I had distracted myself from my feelings with busy-ness, addictive substances and behaviors, and other defense mechanisms. Years of this frenetic inner and outer activity took a tremendous toll on body and mind. When I first dreamt of Paul in 1984, I wanted to track him down and apologize for my callous behavior. I would still be delighted to accomplish this but attempts to find him have been unsuccessful.

Apologizing or making amends is an important aspect of accepting responsibility for our actions. Admitting a wrongdoing and receiving forgiveness from another brings a great deal of relief. However, the most important part of the amends process is finally forgiving oneself, for that is the only way ultimate peace can be found. While working with this dream it occurred to me that, if it was a response to the incubated question, then before my body could completely heal I must experience the relief of self-forgiveness. The dream seems to say that *when I make amends* to Paul *then I* can *hang out* with Vic, a goal established by psyche with the first reunion dream thirty years before this piece.

There was so much charge to the literal interpretation of this *Amends* dream that I didn't go to the intrapersonal level of looking at Paul as a part of myself. Instead, I evoked the processes I had learned to apply to others with whom face-to-face amends are not possible (such as the dead or those who would be hurt by such confrontation). I wrote several letters to Paul even though I could not mail them. I imagined finding Paul and apologizing in person by explaining what I now know about my reasons for my hurtful behavior. I began putting Paul in my daily meditation sessions and imagined that I could send these amends to him through the air. As I did so, dreams about other experiences surfaced, calling for additional amends and self-forgiveness.

Some of these dreams could be acted upon and all brought a great deal of relief and freedom from the fear of hurting others in the future. I was beginning to see that, at one level, illness had served to protect me from the dangers of intimate personal relationships. As long as the "Elephant Woman" syndrome continued, I was protected from physical closeness with everyone. That being the case, I could not hurt others as I had in the past. Thus, continuing illnesses protected me from the intense pain of appropriate guilt.

I was beginning to identify many reasons for being ill as this work proceeded. Seeing the ways in which illness had kept a part of me safe and finding alternative means of safety were essential to my healing.

After ten years of working with forgiveness through a psychospiritual self-teaching program called *A Course in Miracles*, this next piece was received as a profound blessing. This dream is the second part of the "Town Reunion" dream presented in the previous chapter.

Apology from the Soul   MAY 3, 1994

I'm in the reunion hall with others from my high school. Someone sits next to me on the bench. I feel myself going faint when I see it is Paul. I touch his arm and say, "Hello, Paul." When he recognizes me he cringes in mock horror saying something like, "Holy cow! God save me!"

I know he's reacting to the shameful way I left him. I had hoped the experience had been long forgotten but, from his intense recoil, this is not the case. With great seriousness I ask if he will grant me just five minutes of private conversation. He does so without hesitation. We leave the gathering.

We're squeezing through a small space like a tiny path between a building and a bush. It is raining as hard as I am crying. I apologize from my soul for callously leaving him as I did. I am trying to explain to him the reason for my shoddy behavior. I tell him sincerely that he was one of the most uncon-ditionally loving and wonderful men of my life and I cannot express the grief I caused myself by treating him as I did. He says nothing during all this time. He is listening intently and holding a cloth over my head to protect me from the rain.

I was simultaneously puzzled and delighted by this dream. I awoke feeling shaky but very *mature*. When strong feelings are the residual of a dream I always include the feeling in the interpretive work. The shaky feeling I could understand but why would a sense of maturity accompany making amends? Ah, yes. Isn't accepting responsibility for one's actions and one's life a sign of maturity? When I have the desire to whine "It's not *my* fault," I can always detect an inner child hoping to escape the consequences of her actions. Identifying with her creates a sense of powerlessness confounded by a fear of being unable to cope. In contrast, approaching the issue squarely produces a deep sense of pride which, for me, results in peace. This seems to come from tapping into another level of the self that can cope with whatever I have done, learn from it, and choose differently in the future. That seems a good definition of maturity.

What if Paul, as identified in this dream, represents an unconditionally loving energy which I rejected and abandoned? Surely a deeply-felt reconnection with that element of the self would cause a dramatic inner change. Perhaps true healing can result only from unconditional self-acceptance.

Why does this scene follow recognition of the *Disreputable Vic* in the *Town Reunion* Dream? Again Vic and Paul are together as in the *Amends and Connections* dream. If it's possible to make the jump from one scene to another this might be a valid reading: *When* I see an unhealed energy caught in the past *(still lives in the old home town) then* I must boldly confront my former mistakes. This results in a sense of growing up, of maturing.

Another take on this dynamic could be: In order to heal the disreputable former self I must confront and forgive the past. This seems to be an important strand of the web that grounds the powerful energy that needs to be freed.

Guilt and shame strangle the soul and corrode the arteries of creativity and optimism. By presenting us with mirrors reflecting the shadows we would prefer to ignore, psyche provides the most powerful tool for healing and transformation.

INNER EXPLORATION
When/Then

- Sometimes the dream presents a *when/then* statement or dynamic which can be very revealing. It may show up in the content of the material: *When* one thing happens, *then* another follows. Using metaphoric language to describe this often will expose an important truth.

- This dynamic may be seen from scene to scene in a dream. See if it fits the last dream you wrote in your journal. Work each scene in isolation, as if it were the complete dream. Then string two scenes together with the *when/then* statement. If it fits you will get a "body hit!"

Resistance to Shadow Material

- In the last chapter we looked at some forms of dream resistance. Now we turn our attention to a very valid ego defense, that of disowning the shadow.

- Check for really despicable people in your dreams. (Remember that dreams often exaggerate.) Describe the character with five or more adjectives.

- Now pull on your Suit of Honesty and see how those descriptors might fit you in some way. This may be subtle. You may not be acting out what you see in the dream, but may be thinking or feeling what is portrayed, thus doing harm to yourself or, passively, to others.

- Often we hide our best as well as our worst traits from our conscious awareness. So check your dreams for really wonderful characters. Assign adjectives to them and see if you can own those definitions for yourself in some way.

CHAPTER FIFTEEN

Connections

If we study our dreams over a period of time, we begin to see meaningful connections between them. There seems to be an overall guiding force at work steering each of us toward our own unique destiny.

Marie-Louise von Franz in
The Way of the Dream by Frasier Boa

One of the strangest repetitive elements of the entire Victor series is the feeling in most dreams that I have never before made connection with Vic. The word *finally* appears over and over: "I *finally* see Vic," or "Vic and I *finally* talk." This dynamic intrigues me because, aside from the Victor series, while dreaming I often compare one dream to another. I seem to have a *dream consciousness* between dreams which does not extend to this series.

The following three dreams, presented chronologically, deal with this need to connect with the Victor energy in various ways.

Finally Telling Victor   AUGUST 31, 1990

I'm with many other people in a large room at the Air Force Academy. Suddenly I see Vic in front of me and, as in a close-up camera zoom lens shot, I see his face in detail and am thrilled. I call his name and he joins me.

Now Vic and I are sitting together on the floor in this same room. I tell him the entire dream story. He listens, enraptured, not interrupting, and needing no clarification. He's fascinated but not impressed that he is the star of the series. I'm delighted to have the opportunity to tell him the whole story at last.

This was the dream of a woman who finally had found what she had been seeking. She's found it in a place where flying is taught *(Air Force Academy)*. What better place to retrain an immobilized eagle!

The Air Force Academy is a powerful place from my past. Perhaps that's why psyche chose this place as the setting for a dream in which dream ego first told Victor about the dream history. In my junior and senior years of high school I dated cadets at the Air Force Academy, an exciting environment for a young woman. Three of my friends created a stuffed animal mascot for me which I kept and enjoyed for many years. Named AFA, it looked like a very fat, sweet, loving, eagle—though the Air Force Academy mascot was actually the falcon.

Telling the whole story, a process seen in several dreams in this series, is an important part of the recovery and healing process. Through the telling both catharsis and insight are experienced. Each time I've told my personal story to another I have felt lighter and less full, as if the telling allows space for the newly forming self to settle. In this dream the story is told in a very grounded way, while sitting on the *floor*. Reflecting upon that detail allowed me to identify and value my *groundedness* as I relentlessly pursued whatever was necessary to release the eagle to *fly*.

The next dream, one of my favorites of the entire series, reminds me of a stunning experience I had in 1983 when illness was my only awareness and despair my primary emotion. Though I barely had enough energy to read, I was startled by this concept which sustained me enough to continue the struggle. At the same time that the statement numbed my brain it struck a profound chord of truth in my heart. I read, *"Hope is the memory of the future."*

I've often contemplated that paradox since then, always alert to ideas that might substantiate or clarify its meaning. Recently I read about the work of astronomer Fred Hoyle in Fred Alan Wolf's remarkable book, *The Dreaming Universe*. Hoyle suggests that "the future *determines* which choice occurs in the present. Somewhere out there in time yet to be lies the reason and cause of the events that take place now."

At some level I think the long yellow cord in this amazing next dream represents both of these ideas.

Very Long, Powerful Connection   FEBRUARY 11, 1992

I'm visiting high school girl friends, telling them about the wild Victor Biento dream series. Jeanie gets very excited and

> *encourages me to call Vic long distance. I'm too embarrassed*
> *to do so, fearing that he won't remember me. So Jeanie*
> *boldly calls and introduces me to him.*
>
> *When I take the phone I'm thrilled to finally be mak-*
> *ing contact and delight in telling him about the dream his-*
> *tory. He's laughing and enjoying the story as I tell it.*
>
> *I suddenly realize that I'm outside, walking on a lovely*
> *country road with many other people. As we talk I am un-*
> *rolling the longest telephone cord in existence! I could walk for*
> *miles with this cord! The cord is actually a large, bright yel-*
> *low cable. I laugh about this as I report the fact to Vic. He says*
> *it's his cord. He got it from a friend, a telephone repairman!*

From this wonderful piece we see that *the phone on which I am speaking is powered by* Victor's *cord.* What is it to reach a force or energy using the power supplied by the very source being sought? Thinking of this creates a circle in my mind, a sense of reaching out to something that is reaching back to me.

I shared the dream with a friend who said, "Oh, that reminds me of the title of the book I'm reading now: *That Which You are Seeking is Causing You to Seek!*"

At the time of this piece, dream ego had been seeking and learning from a dream character named Victor Biento for more than thirty-one years. This dream says that the powerful cable with which she reaches him comes from him. It doesn't exactly say that what I have been seeking has been seeking me, but it does say that the object of my search provides the means for me to reach it.

The dream says that a bold excited energy (*Jeanie*) must overcome dream ego's embarrassment and reticence *before* any connection can be made. It feels to me as if this shyness is more than a poor sense of self. I think it is the undeveloped self moving into manifestation one tentative step at a time. I wonder if a sense of shyness, timidity, and embarrassment must be overcome if we are to reach the truly profound transpersonal elements of life attempting to reach us. The dream also says that dream ego's ability to be mobile and verbal in the collective (*walk the road with others*) is supplied by Victor. Does this relate to the obvious expansion of my work? Perhaps it can be generalized to mean taking the journey of life.

The following quote from one of America's foremost dream researchers, Robert Van de Castle (*Our Dreaming Mind*), perfectly describes the feelings I experienced with this remarkable piece.

> When one gets in touch with the archetype of the Self, one senses that some larger creative force is leading the way, as though a hidden plan were being followed. Each new discovery of things intricately "coming together" brings forth fresh feelings of surprise and appreciation.

INNER EXPLORATION
Transpersonal Dreams

- Transpersonal dreams extend beyond the usual personal sense of self and of the world. Such dreams, which expose us to profound possibility, are to be treasured.

- Have you experienced a dream in which you felt a greater sense of yourself? Perhaps you were able to fly, thereby seeing a broader and higher perspective of the world. Maybe you met a great spiritual teacher or a powerful historic person. You might have been able to suddenly understand or know something which deeply affected you in the dream. What have these dreams brought to you? How did you feel after the dream?

- Have you enjoyed a dream in which you were able to accomplish feats impossible in awake life? I once wrote a symphony in a dream, clearly hearing all of the voices of the orchestra as I meticulously wrote the score on dozens of sheets of paper. I was exhilarated and amazed for days after this experience as I do not know how either to read or write music.

- When you have such a dream as this consider celebrating or honoring it in some significant way. Once a Jewish friend of mine dreamed of meeting Jesus. She loved him dearly in the dream and was surprised that the feeling held true for many days. Shortly thereafter she found an artist's rendition of Jesus which very much appealed to her. She keeps it in her bedroom much to the amusement of her family and satisfaction of her soul.

- When someone shares a very important dream with you, treat it with the respect reserved for a great master. Perhaps you can help them celebrate the piece in some way.

CHAPTER SIXTEEN

Expansion

It appears that to make sense of the world we must deal with two lives: the sleeping/dreaming life and the waking life. We dream to make sense of the world, to form our maps. We awaken to experience the world, to test our maps by going out into the territory.

Fred Alan Wolf, *The Dreaming Universe*

Throughout this book I have been working from the premise that extricating the eagle from the web has been the combined goal of my psyche and my conscious self. Believing that to be true, and following the lead of my dreams, I have identified many strands that ensnared this imaged creature. But here is a question not yet asked: "For what purpose must this eagle be released?" It is obvious that it will die if it remains in the web, and thus must be freed to survive. Then what?

Here I run the same risk as Icarus, the mythic character destroyed by delusions of grandeur, by an ego problem called *inflation*. How grandiose to identify with a creature as symbolically powerful as an eagle!

True. But wait a minute! *I*, the person I know myself to be, did *not* choose this characterization. Psyche did. My ego-self rejects association to "eagleness." I like the ground and cozy little places with roaring fires, books, a few well-chosen friends, and hot tea and cookies consumed under the weight of several lap cats. An occasional trip to Machu Picchu is food for the eyes and the soul but I want to return to my quiet garden and ocean walks before much time passes. Hang out with eagles? Not likely!

Yet, like it or not, my dreamer continues to connect me to the eagles. In one dream I'm driving up an intricately curving, very steep mountain road. I notice that the few residents of this mountain are busily reconstructing their homes, as if after a disaster. I shout support to all I pass, thinking how brave of them to continue to live here.

Eventually the road shrivels into a footpath, forcing me to abandon the car and walk, something I clearly must do. I trudge ahead, ever focused on the top of the mountain. After many treacherous dream hours I arrive at the summit and am rewarded by an utterly spectacular view spreading hundreds of miles. Suddenly I am frightened by an unfamiliar, awesome, terrifying sound and cling to a nearby boulder. I feel enormous pressure followed by a blackout of the light. Looking up, I see, hear, and feel the eagle as he moves off the mountain into the vast unknown. I weep with awe and joy.

This dream was a memorable experience which suggested not only survival after the crisis *(rebuilding the homes)*, but also enormous hope for achieving the personal freedom I had sought for so many years. Truthfully, only at rare times do I feel such potent freeing energy within me. Abraham Maslow defined these as *peak experiences*, times when one is beyond oneself, transcended for a few moments, hours, even a day or two, before the density of mundane life presses one to earth again. Everyone has these rarefied *eagle-like* experiences now and again. But what would it be like to *be* an eagle, soaring day after day? No thanks, too expansive for me.

The expansive aspect of eagleness reminds me of a set of five dreams which influenced my decision to end my teaching career. All of them had to do, in a variety of ways, with being in aircraft which crashed because of flying too low! At one level the images related to an eagle's ability and necessity to fly high, to expand, to soar.

Eagleness will be different for each person working with this symbol (or totem animal, as my Native American friends identify it). I've heard perhaps a dozen eagle dreams from as many clients and, as is generally true of those who dream of animal symbols, all the dreamers were deeply impacted by their material. It is likely that they are being connected to a similar kind of energy. Yet each dreamer's need for such power or vision is as different as each of our journeys and ultimate life goals.

Two other aspects of eagleness are suggested by astrological and Native American symbology. Reading that Carl Jung was interested in astrology led me to wonder about my chart and the innate characteristics it might reveal. During my first astrological reading I was told that I am a Scorpio—no surprise to anyone I stung in my venomous past. I learned that growth and development are possible within the ancient astrological system and that the evolved

Scorpio transforms into an eagle! In addition, Native Americans see the eagle as a symbol of spirit. Jamie Sams and David Carson in *Medicine Cards* present it this way:

> Eagle medicine is the power of the Great Spirit, the connection to the Divine. It is the ability to live in the realm of spirit, and yet remain connected and balanced within the realm of Earth. Eagle soars, and is quick to observe expansiveness within the overall pattern of life. From the heights of the clouds, Eagle is close to the heavens where the Great Spirit dwells.

What does eagleness mean in my trek? At the mundane level, I think others in my life see it more easily and clearly than I. For ten months before the next dream I had been pressured by friends, clients, and associates to expand my private practice. At the same time I had dreams about playing in symphony orchestras and big league basketball teams. It felt as if forces beyond my divining were demanding that I "spread my wings" beyond my safe, cozy, very private life. My weekly public radio dream show had begun and was pushing me to my limits of exposure. I had begun training an energetic band of aspiring dream professionals in a two-year program in nearby Santa Cruz, which invited additional dreamwork across the Monterey Bay. One part of me was flying off cliffs while another was seriously resistant to this process, as the following dreams clearly express. Here we see an *expansion/contraction* dynamic contained within two dreams on the same night.

Clutching and Controlling   AUGUST 15, 1991

I'm climbing up the nearly vertical stairs of a slide. The slide is shiny, long and curving. At the top of the slide I debate going down. Yikes! What have I gotten myself into!? Maybe I should bail over the side. If I do that, everyone will think I'm a nerdy chicken. I could surreptitiously climb back down but that is really the coward's way out. What a dilemma!

What would Victor do here, I wonder.

Oh, what the hell, let's go for it! I climb on and let go but almost immediately experience the desire to control both the speed and exhilaration of the ride. Will I burn my hands if I grab the railings? I do so and slow down but I lose the thrill and self-pride. Again I think of Victor Biento and feel ashamed of myself.

Why would I think of Vic in this place of indecision and fearful control? Why am I willing to climb *up and on* but then abandon the process by hanging on tightly? These were my thoughts as I examined this dream between REM cycles. Perhaps the next dream (same night) answers those queries.

Stingy Gardener   AUGUST 15, 1991 (CONTINUED)

I'm tending the garden of a place where groups meet. I joyfully plant a young rose bush against a wall on the first level of this multitiered teaching place.

One day I notice that something is different in my garden. I find that my precious rose bush has been transplanted into a pot and brought up to the second level. People are sitting around admiring and loving the rose but I'm very upset. I want the rose to be with me downstairs.

I go into the kitchen to complain to the woman in charge. I tell the woman my problem with the rose bush. She offers me solace but is clearly disappointed in me.

I feel cheap and petty but I want the rose bush for myself! Finally I decide that I'll bring the rose down to my level in the morning and take it upstairs for the afternoon sun, thereby serving the needs of everyone. Now that it's in a pot it can be moved. This is a great solution.

As often happens in my dream life, one dream presents the problem and another clarifies it. In the first piece dream ego is *willing to climb aboard but is unwilling to really let go.* I think dream two brilliantly shows why.

Like the process of human growth, a *rose* is a beautiful creation which unfolds one petal at a time. Eventually, with passage of enough time, its wholeness is seen. I could resonate to this characterization with my actual sense of personal development in my life and the growth of my career in the dream field. However, I was stuck and *unwilling to let go* (slide images) because (jump to second dream) a self-protective, controlling aspect of my personality did not want to move, *to be taken to a higher level.* Instead, I wanted to remain solitary and protected by the wall. However, the dream says that through the process of *transplanting* I had become willing to compromise.

This certainly reflected my feelings regarding my dream teaching practice, Dream Dance tapes, and the radio show. I felt a need to protect my boundaries (stay close to my walls), stay on the same level and to keep my growth to myself. Though it's often a healthy thing to do, I needed to see that self-protection could result in pettiness and a sense of personal stinginess, as in being unable to "share" the growth.

The image of *the second level, a higher level,* cracked this piece for me. I had always felt *high* from doing dreamwork but I had never seen that the act of sharing that work takes me to a higher level or place of consciousness. The dream says that *serving the needs of the collective* (the people on the second level who wanted the rose) does exactly that. Consciously making that connection *physically released the tension in my body.* I literally could feel a shift from *contraction to expansion* with that awareness from the dream.

Though dream ego's feelings are powerfully felt in this dream, they are the feelings of the unhealed self. It's the patterned part of me I knew well. To identify only with dream ego's feelings would have been a deadly reconstruction of the web, as she represents the stuck place beyond which the dream is gently pushing. That healing perspective resides in *the woman in charge.*

The *woman in charge* certainly represents the leading energy in my psyche. Although the woman in charge is unwilling to support dream ego's immobility, she is sympathetic.

Deciding that I needed more information to understand this piece, I engaged in an active imagination, telling the woman: "I cannot possibly let the rose bush go to the second level. I worked so hard on its growth. It needs the wall to protect it from the wind." I hear my whiny voice in my head as I try to make the woman understand and agree.

She will not. She continues to work while saying that she understands my fear of movement but she will not agree that the rose should remain in the ground. "It must move to the people and the sun. That is best for the plant, for the others and for you, too. You need to enjoy the growth you have tended at a higher level with more people."

I was clearly ready to hear from this element of my psyche because the shift in my attitude from whiny fear to exhilarated possibility was immediate. After this work I felt no need to *cling to the sides* of either the slide or the wall. I was readily willing to say *yes* to new opportunities, in both the awake world and my dreams.

In addition, the ability to release, to move, to expand has spiritual meaning for me. It is an act of surrender and trust in the unknown which has been a major element of my overall recovery from my first healing experience with the Eagle Dream. I like the way Jacquelyn Small says it in her book, *Transformers: The Artists of Self Creation*:

> "I surrender" is an inner act of letting go, a willed action of getting out of the way so that the truth can come in. The "me" who surrenders is a little ego-dominated me who thought she had to run the show. Now the "I" who manifests my God-nature in the world, my true Self, can take over. I follow the dictates of the higher Self, who receives its power directly from the Source where all truth resides.

If a person hopes to recover from the ravages of substance or relationship abuse, s/he must make contact with a part of the self which is not addicted. Then the addict must be willing to turn his/her power over to that healthy energy. This dynamic may be identified as the *higher power.* Beyond that comes a sense of *connection* to a universal power or movement that supports life, growth, fulfillment, and service.

To remain sane and sober, and to free myself from my *addiction* to illness, I had to make a commitment to a power beyond my ego. This is often expressed as *turning oneself over* and *surrendering to a power greater than the self.* This can be done only if the ego is willing to let go of control, a major step for anyone in recovery. Only then are other universal forces able to participate in our process. As Julia Cameron writes in *The Artist's Way,* "It is my experience both as an artist and a teacher that when we move out on faith into the act of creation, the universe is able to advance. It's a little like opening a gate at the top of a field irrigation system. Once we remove the blocks the flow moves in."

In the vernacular of my *Clutching and Controlling* dream, *to get on the slide and release all control* is an example of such a process. I was surprised by how untrusting dream ego was when confronted with the issue of expansion in this piece. That fearful aspect of self must be dealt with empathetically. Change *can be* forced upon this resistant element by *"should-ing"* or *threatening,* but that kind of change seldom will be permanent. Instead, we must relate to the fear, embrace it, let it express itself through dialogue and other means, and gently show the options that are possible. Over time, when dealt with in this loving fashion, the resistance dissolves like tension during a series of massage therapy sessions.

The ability to release this tightness, the tight reins of the ego, and turn oneself over to the wider, broader, deeper dimensions of the whole self or of psyche is required if important growth is to result from dreamwork. Until I am willing to challenge dream ego's strong opinions and feelings within a dream, I am simply serving the status quo of my former patterns and original script. When I look for, acknowledge, and comply with the differing per-spectives of other dream characters I am more likely to embrace the essence of the dream.

The previous dreams occurred one week before Dream Dance Company's first audio-set was placed on the market. The day after that I flew to Europe to lead workshops in Germany and Austria. Expansion? Indeed! The following dream shows the success of those expanding experiences and continues the psychic massage that loosened old fears that otherwise might have contracted my willingness to expand.

Spectacular Old Building in Vic's Town
OCTOBER 11, 1991

Mother and I are traveling through the town where Vic Biento lives. We stop to have lunch in a fascinating old build-ing, a former monastery. The old building is being restored to its original splendor. I enter a corridor of intricately carved wooden walls displaying spectacular old works of art.

Now I'm looking down on a large room. From above, I have a clear overview of this two-hundred-person lecture hall in a gently curved room with easy chairs tiered top to bottom as if enfolding the stage. I'm delighted to see an enormous fire-place at the back of the stage. This gives the audience the cozy view of a huge fire while the onstage speakers can feel the lovely warmth and support from behind.

With my bird-like perspective I can see down into the back-stage area. It is a formal library with another beautiful fire-place warming the book-lined walls. I'm thoroughly enchanted.

As Mother and I leave the building I imagine that some-one may recognize me now that the tapes are out. For the first

*time I realize I might like that. I'm very happy to know that
this lovely restaurant/lecture forum exists where Vic lives.*

To be in the *town where Vic lives* is to be in the collective place *(town)* which contains what I have been seeking all these years *(Vic)*. Associating to the *collective* led me to focus on career or societal issues. In my case, they are the same, since I feel strongly that teaching people to understand dreams very positively impacts society.

The mother in this dream is healthy and happy. Therefore, I'm traveling with a healed nurturing force instead of the emotionally and physical fragile martyr/victim of old. We're being nourished *(eating)* in a space which is being restored to its original spiritual magnificence *(monastery)*. This connects to taking the rose to the higher level in the sun. It also relates to the eagle as a Native American symbol for spiritual attainment and power.

The focus that psyche provides is the overview of the lecture forum, the teaching place (an environment similar to that in the *Stingy Gardener* dream). If this refers to *my* teaching, this is a view I have never imagined. Could it really be possible to do this work in the larger collective as I do it with my little practice now, surrounded by warmth, support, and beauty? The dream's message—that this is what exists *where Vic lives*—provided a powerful feeling of encouragement.

Perhaps you have noticed in your own life that when you move into a new venture you suddenly are put in contact with many people doing the same thing. This is one of the many ways I experience *warmth and support in a renovated spiritual place.* This phenomenon seems to manifest when I have said *yes* to a new venture which serves the collective in some way. Thus it was that I began to meet many authors and tape producers who willingly shared their experiences of being in the realm shown in the dream: on stage, up front, surrounded by the public. Over and over I heard of the fears that these creative people had overcome to produce and promote their work. The stories about pleasant and intelligent interviewers and receptive audiences have been most encouraging to my resistant, homebody self. The dream clearly promised that being in a public speaking environment need not be cold *(fireplaces)*, stupid *(library backstage)*, or even mundane *(former monastery)*. That all this reconstruction and exquisite beauty existed *in the place where Vic lives* further supported expansion into the public domain.

If dreams form our maps, as suggested by Fred Alan Wolf, this dream creates a beautiful, supportive, expanded teaching environment. Being able to test its accuracy depends on my ability to let go in trust, share my growth and move to higher levels. In this light I see each of these three dreams as attempting to extricate the eagle from the restrictions of the web.

It feels more and more that the Vic Biento energy in my psyche is retraining that grounded, dying creature and encouraging it to fly, to mingle more broadly in the collective, and to be at home in the realm of the spirit.

INNER EXPLORATION

Dream Animals

- Animals in dreams usually generate a great deal of feeling within the dreamer. Fear, awe, love, and delight are common responses.

- When an animal appears in your dreams, associate with it in the same ways you would relate to a person or place. Describe it. Define it. Write about the attributes of the creature, what it eats, where it lives, and what its social behaviors tend to be.

- If you have personal history with this type of animal, recall and write about that. If the animal is or was your pet describe its personal idiosyncrasies, for every pet is unique. Does the description remind you of any person or any part of yourself?

- If the animal is unfamiliar to you, do some research about it. (I very much like two particular resources for animal information: *Animal-Speak* by Ted Andrews and *The Medicine Cards* by Jamie Sams and David Carson.)

- If the dream presented the animal in a favorable light, wonder what gift this kind of creature could bring to you. If the animal frightens you, wonder what kind of power or characteristics you might be afraid of in yourself or in others.

- If the dream strongly affected you, collect pictures of the animal. Draw or paint it. Look for such creatures in the awake world. Find stuffed animals, jewelry, or statues of the animal. In this way you bring the power of the animal to live with you. You become more integrated with it. Your future dreams will reflect this integration.

CHAPTER SEVENTEEN

Contraction

While much cause of human suffering can be traced to negligent fostering, there is also within the psyche naturally an innate *contra naturam* aspect, an "against nature" force. The *contra naturam* aspect opposes the *positive*: it is *against development, against harmony, and against the wild.* It is a derisive and murderous antagonist that is born into us, and even with the best parental nurture the intruder's sole assignment is to attempt to turn all crossroads into closed roads. [*emphasis added*]

Clarissa Pinkola Estés, Ph.D.
Women Who Run With the Wolves

I t has been my experience that an act of expansion or freedom calls forth an opposite force determined to contract and control. The impetus of this restricting power is not as benign as a pendulum's balancing swing. This is not mere homeostatic reluctance, which can be gentled into change by transforming fear into action. I experience this determined contracting energy as *opposed to* healing, to development, and to both personal and collective evolution. The following dreams exposed this drive powerfully enough for me to escape its destructive intent.

Boxed in by Nazis   JUNE 30, 1990

I've written Vic, telling him about the Victor Biento Dream Series in preparation for seeing him face-to-face. When I get to his house, several Nazi-type fraus keep me in an anteroom. They simply tell me that I can't see Vic. They stand like immovable boulders. Clearly there is no way around them. I'm very upset and extremely frustrated. I am hopelessly unable to reach Victor.

On the morning of the dream I recorded this response in my journal: "This force feels more collective than personal, as I think of *Nazi* as a banding-together of energy which protects its supposed superiority by vicious, well-organized destruction. Clearly a powerful energy is determined to keep me from *facing* Victor. What is it to tell Victor about the dream series and what repressive intrapsychic force is determined to disallow this telling?"

I couldn't answer these two questions at that time, for I did not yet consciously understand the significance of the Victor Biento Dream Series. Not until well into the research for this book could I see the goal of the series to extricate me from the myriad strands of the life-taking web. It felt as if repressive forces, perhaps those which had originally imprisoned the eagle, did not want the growth process to continue at the time of this dream.

On the morning of the dream I employed a process to counteract the destructive energy of the Nazis in the dream. I released the need to intellectually understand the content of the dream by reassuring myself that the meaning would unfold in the future. I examined the dream to identify the contracting, negative force. Then I made a conscious commitment to disallow this repressive Nazi force a free hand, so to speak. In this case, all I could do was put my conscious self on alert for repressing, controlling, murdering thoughts or behaviors determined to keep me from "facing Victor," from reaching that which I had so long sought.

During the next few days I held the image of the Nazi fraus before me. Focusing on them allowed me to visualize a dictatorial, controlling aspect of my physical illnesses. I felt that for years I had been kept in the anteroom of life, separated from what I really wanted. Food and environmental allergies isolated me from the world and its options. After one severe attack I had a phone consultation with a Los Angeles physician specializing in immune system deficiencies. He told me that I should strip my house of all padded substances, get rid of all animals and plants, have organic food delivered to my door, and see no one except my doctor for six months.

In shock, I hung up the phone to consider his suggestion. I saw an image of me backing into a cave from which I would never escape. I felt a whoosh of energy surge upward, igniting a flame of determination. "NO," I screamed, "That's going the wrong way! I will not withdraw anymore!" Today I'm convinced that was a pivotal decision in reversing the physical pattern of contraction and repression. I strongly believe that following that well-meaning doctor's advice would have caused the eagle to die in the web. I am deeply grateful for the energy that rebelled against that suggestion and the will that allowed me to manifest the decision.

The following dream took many days to unravel. The effort was fully rewarded when the message was received. Again, the need to tell about the Victor Series is thwarted.

Robert Substitutes for the Murderer

I'm visiting Robert in an empty gymnasium. I'm excited to tell him about the Vic Biento series but he is clearly disinterested. We are walking around and around the perimeter of the gym. Robert tells me he has been chosen to take Barton's place because Barton has been convicted of murder.

Robert's preoccupation with his new role makes him oblivious to the dream series and to what is important and valuable for me. We continue to walk around the outside, going nowhere near the center of either the room or my dream series.

As an associate and I worked on this dream we marveled at psyche's ability to choose the explicitly perfect symbols of *Robert* and *Barton*. At first my memory was vague as I worked to remember each of these characters from my past. Finally I realized that both were precisely necessary to exemplify what I needed to understand.

I recalled both Barton and Robert as tragically wasted individuals. Ten years before this dream Robert had been a fellow participant in a gestalt therapy group. He was a handsome man with a strong personality and a great deal of verbal and creative talent. When introducing himself to the group, he said he could clearly see who he wanted to become but he could never reach that image. I was fascinated when he worked in the group because he tried many ways to disarm, charm, and even bully the therapists. Each time he began to feel his pain he would stand up and leave the room. Neither of the therapists in the program could help him confront his issues. I was amazed by how much awareness Robert had of his process. He verbalized that rather than work through his issues he preferred to deal with his misery by getting drunk seven days a week and cheating on his wife. During the year that we worked together he never budged from this position, which I considered pathetically stuck.

On the other hand, Barton did manifest his ideal image by becoming influential and famous in his field. Everyone who knew him was stunned when, during a wild, designer drug weekend, Barton murdered an associate. Now he is a literal prisoner, as Robert is a psychological one. Both powerful energies are locked up, unable to live freely. Seeing them both together in one dream severely jolted me. The dream said that due to these two energies I could not voice the Victor Biento Series. I therefore saw this material as very threatening and spent many hours working on it with several associates.

I realized that to visit Robert was to be in a scared, sick, stuck, place of undeveloped potential. Being in the gym suggested the psychological games he always played. To *walk the perimeter, going around and around*, showed the process of not getting to the center or core of either issues or self. As long as I walk this way, no attention will be paid to the importance of the messages from Victor.

I had not consciously thought of the man called Barton for fifteen years. I learned of him while participating in a training program in the 1970s. As I recall the story, he exemplified the consummate entrepreneur. His genius had created an original structure of thought resulting in the renovation of his field. The murdered associate was in charge of *Research and Development!* Recalling that fact shook me like a 6.0 earthquake because, at the time of this dream, I was considering abandoning my *research* about the Vic series.

For several months I had been conflicted about submitting my first proposal to speak about the Victor dream series at an international dream conference. I was experiencing a great deal of doubt about exposing this apparently important yet still not fully understood *research* in such a public environment. This dream showed me that walking as Robert did would keep me from the core of my issues and from the center of myself. I would thus be unable to voice the importance of this vital dream series.

I concluded that not doing the kind of deep psychological work that Robert had always avoided rendered me as sick as he was. I could then identify two components to my particular form of illness. First, at the time of the dream I was miserable because the staph infection which plagued me for eight years was not responding to antibiotics. It continued to flare up at least once a month. Though not as disfiguring as in former years, it hampered my personal sense of acceptability and, therefore, my activities. This resulted in the second illness, that of a shameful sense of self perfectly represented by the ugly mask of the staph infection.

Hypnosis was the only therapy I hadn't yet pursued which might be able *to get to the center or the core.* Thus, I began a series of remarkable hypnosis treatments with a talented medical doctor. Each session surprised us both with the intensity of the deeply buried pain we uncovered. (During each session I was able to empathize more completely with Robert's need to escape his pain!) In the most astonishing session I found myself locked in deadly conflict within my mother's womb. I felt seriously threatened there and desperately wanted to get out. But I was equally fearful of facing what awaited me outside. This dilemma of imprisonment produced the same kind of horror as the Eagle Dream. In each case I experienced the anguish and grief of living beings trapped and unable to move.

Victor's Healing Embrace, the powerful dream in which Victor accepts me despite the ugliness of the staph infection, had been providing healing for six months before the hypnotherapy. The additional conscious work related to the profound session in the womb took several more weeks to complete. I have had no significant staph outbreaks since. To this writing that is a period of eight years.

In June 1992 I presented a paper about the Victor Biento dreams at an important professional conference. It was enthusiastically received and generated a great deal of excitement. As a result, a magazine writer requested an interview about the Victor Biento series. The writer, a successful novelist, was so effusive in his excitement about the import of the series that I began seriously contemplating writing a book about the Biento dreams.

Though this seemed a logical next step, I had no idea how to accomplish such a task. Lecturing, teaching, and broadcasting are all easy for me but I didn't see myself possessing the tenacity, skill, or discipline to produce a book. I couldn't imagine how to create the necessary time for such a horrendous project. I neither owned nor knew how to operate a computer. My logical, awake self found the entire notion too preposterous and overwhelming to seriously consider. And then this dream.

Getting Vic off the Bus   JULY 22, 1992

I'm helping some preteen boys get off a stationary bus/classroom. I see that many children have already made it, but young Victor is unable to get out. He wants me to stay and hold him during the night. He's scared and feels inadequate because he can't get off the bus.

If I tend to him by holding and accepting him, he'll try to get down again tomorrow. I clearly imagine how it would feel to hold him, as he wants. It feels good; I, too, will be healed as I do this for him. I agree.

Then he shyly asks if I'll leave him when he falls asleep. I'm shocked by the question as I intend to stay and hold him for the entire night. He's relieved and delighted that I won't abandon him.

My journal records this response: "Seeing Victor in this needy and vulnerable place is really scary. My feelings of tenderness and commitment to Victor are intensely powerful in the dream. I bring that pledge into this conscious realm and promise not to abandon *Victor* though I do not, at this moment, know what that commitment means."

This is another example of surrendering to the guidance of the dream before my awake ego is able to fully comprehend the material. As I say the words of the dream, a knowing exists in my body which is not yet in my brain. It feels to me that *when* I take the step of commitment *then* the understanding unfolds into consciousness. It's as if I invite the light to shine by simply installing the lamp. The switch of awareness clicks automatically as I go about the day gently reminding myself of the dream. I wait patiently for the *ah ha!* to surface.

So it was with this piece. I shared it with a dream friend who knew nothing about the Victor series. With fresh eyes my friend asked if a *project* might be caught in an undeveloped *(preteen)* state? When I was able to shift Vic from a *psychic energy* to a *project*—at this point the book—the light snapped on immediately. I suddenly saw this thirty-year-long inner relationship moving into physical form. It had the potential of becoming a teaching tool for others as well as myself.

Due to all my fears, Victor, the book, is stuck on the unmoving *(stationary)* place of learning *(classroom)* for the collective *(bus)*. He (the book and the force always propelling me) is fearful of abandonment. Having made my commitment to stay throughout the night (the darkness of the unknown) I know that somehow this project will manifest. Two months later I took my first retreat to begin this book. Alas, that beginning did not still the voice urging contraction, as additional dreams will illustrate.

From clients and radio show callers I hear a common dream theme which exposes feelings of desperation at the loss of the creative process. These dreams frequently cause an examination of the collective demands and prohibitions that destroy authentic, creative self-expression. This issue became the topic of one of my radio shows. As a result, I shared a dream titled *No Pro-Choice* in which dream ego is told by a *pharmacist* that she must vote *against* a Pro-Choice initiative. I loved the metaphor of repression from the part of psyche which *fills the prescriptions of the collective.* (I think this element within us is another example of what Estés means by the *contra naturam* force.)

As I chatted with my audience about the various forms of control which stifle the ability to manifest what one chooses, I flashed on an image of my father in his most imprisoned state. As sometimes happens when I'm on the air, my unconscious seemed to take control of the microphone by telling a story which, in this case, resulted in an adrenalin rush during the telling and a deep feeling of shame when the show was over.

The caller and I were talking about the "prescriptions" each of us had "bought" which destroyed or tempered our creativity. The caller identified the feeling of rage that sometimes exploded into destructive action when he felt totally thwarted creatively. I flashed on my own father's rages and depressions, making the connection to his often told story of "almost making it in the big time."

My dad's great love was music. He began leading bands during the Big Band era in the twenties. In those days the high watermark in the band business was a national radio contract. Dad's band had made it to an audition at a major network. Due to some emergency his lead trumpet player arrived late. The audition was forfeited and Sammy Kaye (Swing and Sway with Sammy Kaye), the next band to play, got the contract.

My dad continued to lead bands, off and on. Unfortunately, he was unable to consistently make a living at his passion and always traded it for jobs he barely tolerated. Indeed, the only memories I have of a healthy, happy, vibrant father come from the times he was involved in the entertainment business.

Most of the rest of the time he was physically ill or lethargic. I suspect he was deeply depressed most of his life.

While telling this story on the air I had two realizations vital to my own creative freedom. First, my family script contained the belief that it is impractical—indeed, impossible—to successfully do what one loves. And then I realized I had already transcended that block. At that very moment, while speaking to my radio caller, I was doing what my father yearned for all his life. I was able to work, to live, my passion full-time. I was even able to realize my father's aspirations to be on the radio.

I experienced a feeling of shame after the show, as often happens with the first telling of a family secret. It's as if exposures of this kind threaten the family script and therefore the homeostasis of the ego. The writing of this book had begun a month earlier, so the old self was being severely challenged. Stirring up the inner self in this way usually produces an important dream. Read on for that night's example.

Family Uproar Causes Victor's Rejection   NOVEMBER 21, 1992

I'm on a retreat with my family. Horrible, ugly, screaming fights ensue between various family members. I'm devastated, chagrined, embarrassed, and ashamed. I want everyone to stop the uproar. In my attempt to deal with this ever-present family problem, I lose control of myself and give up.

Victor is now present. I'm thrilled to see him. I really want to talk to him, to share what's been going on with me as a result of his dream series. But he is unwilling to connect with me. He's disappointed and upset with me. He abandons me and goes off. I'm devastated.

My dream journal records the following:

This dream is as disturbing as a nightmare. I have been extremely anxious all day but couldn't find time to work it until now, 4:00 P.M. I feel enormously threatened by the rejection by Vic, this inner force so important to my growth, to my freedom. I know I must understand what has caused Victor's rejection.

In the first place *to be on retreat* is the phrase I use to describe my time away to write the book. So, *when* I am creating and the negative family dynamic begins, *then* something very important rejects me. That rejection feels like I will lose all I've been working towards for thirty plus years. *No wonder I'm anxious!*

The dream says that *when* I *lose control* and *give up fighting* the typical family dynamic *then* I lose connection to Victor! Yes! That's it! *If* I *stop* fighting my destructive family belief system, *then* I will lose all I've worked towards in freeing the eagle. This is obviously the message psyche wanted me to get because all my anxiety is replaced by excitement!

Our prescriptions for success are contained within our family and cultural scripts. If I lose control and give up fighting the family limitations, Victor will be abandoned on that bus and the eagle will continue its pathetic imprisonment. Victor's disappointment and rejection scared me into the place of realization before that stuckness became permanent.

However, the old tapes have not been played through yet, as the next blocking dream shows.

Wanting to Tell Vic about the Book   AUGUST 5, 1993

My family and I are among a large gathering of people. I see Victor, make contact with him immediately, and enjoy casually chatting with him.

As I prepare my bath I excitedly report this connection to my family. I say that I'll tell Vic about the book tomorrow

*and get his reaction to it. I'm feeling really brave and direct
about this. I'm proud of myself.*

*Mother has a fit! She turns into a crazy person insist-
ing that in no way can I do this! She's maniacal! The rest of
the women in the family agree that I should have no further
contact with Vic.*

*I'm very confused and upset. Damn! I felt so good about
myself for a while! Now I feel ashamed.*

How do we know that dream ego is the example of health in this piece?
Perhaps, from the perspective of the feminine principle (*the women in the family*), there is a valid reason to abandon the public exposure of the Victor series.
Anytime there is a conflict such as this within dream content I seriously examine the dream to determine which opinion or position represents growth and
healing. Two sets of emotions are striking here. First, dream ego feels *brave,
direct, and proud.* These are not usually descriptors of dysfunction. Nor are they
common to this dream series nor my awake sense of self at this time. In reviewing my awake ego's emotions in the presence of something I really want I am
much more likely to feel shy, reticent, and not good enough to make contact.
Thus, the feeling of ease in this dream represents self-acceptance and growth.

On the other hand, after the attack from the *crazy mother* dream ego feels
confused, upset, and ashamed. These are the familiar responses for an ego which
has stepped beyond the bounds of its former self, or of family or cultural
expectations (*prescriptions*) and desires. Again, shame surfaces as a control
mechanism of the past. Therefore, to align my conscious self with the
demands of the family feels retrogressive and contracting, not progressive and
expanding. Following these feelings returns the eagle to the web, a goal of the
old paradigm but clearly not of psyche, to which I must maintain allegiance.

Without work on these dreams would the projects resulting from the Victor Biento series have gone dormant? There is no way to tell, of course, but my guess is yes. By the time a dream like this surfaces I notice that my feelings of passion and commitment for a particular creative work have become dulled, even deadened. The days before such a dream I feel distracted, bored, aimless. I don't remember my goals and desires. Nothing tastes quite right, the Pacific Ocean looks flat, and flowers are odorless. I'm never satisfied with how I look, every activity seems trivial, and nothing is worth the time it takes. Indeed, in this state the murderous forces are in control. Gratefully, a dream always alerts me to the presence of and shows me how to escape from this killer force.

Working each of the dreams presented in this chapter caused a definite perceptual shift, a reawakening of excitement in senses and activity. After each dream I was able to recommit to my goals with renewed desire and productivity. This sense of commitment to the dream and its teaching supports the transformation that wants to occur. Louis Savary puts it this way in "Dreams and Spiritual Energy": "If you don't use the energy released in the dream, it will slip back into the unconscious, and no longer be as readily available."

INNER EXPLORATION

Repressors

• In the dream, *Taming the Rebel* (in Chapter Five), Victor knows only about the repressive force identified as the British Parliament. What forms do such controllers take in your dreams? Nazis? Sadistic cops? A hated mean teacher from grade school? A bully? A dictator? A gang?

• How does dream ego typically respond to the repressive forces? Compliance? Physical attack? Fleeing? What does the response tell you about your ability to deal with internal and external repressors?

• Sometimes a repressor takes on mythic form. For example, a woman unable to get along with female bosses suddenly began dreaming about the wicked stepmother in Cinderella. She identified that fairy tale as her most remembered, but it was her least favorite because she so feared the stepmother. While working on the series the dreamer realized that she automatically assumed that a female in authority would be as cold and wicked as the stepmother.

• Do you remember a childhood fairy tale or story? Who was the repressor in that story? Does that form of controller still operate in your life today?

CHAPTER EIGHTEEN

Process

...addiction itself is romanticized in our culture. Consider the romantic image of the drinking writer or the rock star who is a drug addict. Quite often the early deaths of creative persons suffering from addiction are romanticized, drawing those who admire *creativity* along a similarly addictive path.

Linda Schierse Leonard, *Witness to the Fire*

In retrospect, I am astounded I could let go of the drama of being a suffering artist. Nothing dies harder than a bad idea.

Julia Cameron, *The Artist's Way*

Frequently my dreamer focuses on my ways of *doing* or *thinking*, often activating an alteration of my *process*—in how I feel, think, and act. Adhering to the awarenesses in these process dreams has helped me to work and play with less stress, more productivity, and greater harmony within myself and in partnership with others. The dreams in this chapter are examples from the Victor Biento series which informed and helped to transform specific areas of my creative process.

As I contemplated the demands of writing a book, I confronted the belief that creative types must be at least slightly insane to be productive. "Insanity is to art what garlic is to food," wrote a sage from ancient Greece. Modern culture seems to embrace this notion as well. As I pondered ideas about the creative process, both collective and family beliefs were pushed up to the surface.

Since childhood I had heard that suffering is an absolute necessity for creative people. In addition, our culture seems to value the idea that the creative process is one which cannot be blended into a normal life. In order to produce a book, would I need to cut off an ear or move to an island and drink myself to death? Would I have to suffer mightily to earn the designation of "author?" Would it be impossible to create a book *and* work *and* maintain a social life? Could I write *and* continue to exercise body, mind, and spirit without the use of substances or behaviors that abuse all three?

My concerns about writing a book while maintaining my professional and spiritual practice were resolved by this valuable image in a meditation session: I saw one isolated bead separated from three touching beads. This led me to envision a plan to work with clients for the first three weeks of each month while reserving the last week for writing. Though it seemed plausible I wondered if I could financially and emotionally accomplish this *three-and-one plan*. By this time I had learned that committing to growth and change both activates and dispels fears, so I announced my intention and waited for the responses to surface.

The following advice from Victor occurred a week before my first writing retreat to begin this book. The image it contained allowed me to feel secure in my choice.

Vic Biento and the Embracing Couple

I'm with Vic in a large room. I'm helping him set up a film or slide projector. He is wearing pajamas and I think he is recovering from an illness. We're intently engaged in an important discussion, trying to understand a major philosophical issue or solve a problem.

On a screen Victor projects a picture of a couple in bed. We see the couple from above them. Looking down, I see that they are wrapped in each other's arms, facing each other, not in the spoon position. The man is on the left, the woman on the right. I think they are very much in love. "You should be like that," Vic says. "I'm working on it," I answer. "I'm very willing." Vic continues to deal with the video equipment.

It seemed that the *recovering* Victor in this dream represented my inner healing from compulsive "workaholic" behavior. It felt as if a way to do that was to combine these inner processes so that each could see the other, could know what the other was doing.

In addition, by this time I considered the words *to recover* to mean *to find what had been lost.* Looking at that facet, the Vic energy is *recovering* something in my psyche or awake process that is tender and loving, intimately melding two divergent but supporting forces.

The one who is recovering, who is finding what has been lost, wants dream ego to see the masculine and feminine in relationship. If this is the solution to the problem being discussed, then the entwined, face-to-face relationship between the two is the answer.

I took this image very seriously from my first writing day. As a result, I disregarded all suggestions from writing teachers about structure and discipline. Instead of following advice for the masculine *doer* ("Make yourself write five hours every day, including holidays, whether you want to or not") I checked in with my feminine *feelings* and wrote only when I wanted to, when I felt literally *moved* to do so, when I would be *unhappy* if I didn't write. As emotions surfaced due to the material I was writing, I devoted time and attention to deal with them before proceeding. I gave up all notions of a timeline for the project, and committed myself to working for balance, not for a schedule.

About six months after my first writing week, an observant friend asked how the book was going. I enthusiastically responded with a description of the amazing ability to be totally absorbed in the writing process for a week and then release the project to continue the rest of my life. My friend reported that, as I talked, I had gently inserted and retracted my cupped right fist from the open left hand. As I talked about the writing process the right hand nestled inside the left. When discussing the other activities the right hand was out. I felt an immediate and powerful body hit as the *Embracing Couple* dream image flashed. My hands had formed the image from this dream to describe the process I was living. It seemed I had been spared the fate of the creatively insane and was, indeed, working a program of recovery while creating a useful book.

A little more than a year later we return to issues of the creative process from a different perspective.

Infantile Romanticism   AUGUST 19, 1993

As Sally, Sarah and I hike in the mountains we speculate about the reason for the Victor Biento material. In their usual romantic thinking they suggest that Vic and I actually had a wild romance in high school. They suggest that, for reasons unknown, I have repressed this memory. I am totally irritated with them for their infantile romantic perspective and simplistic literal thinking. Nonetheless, I worry that, if this suggestion is true, the premise of the book will be destroyed. Then I will have to abandon the project I have come to love.

After recording this dream I considered the possibility that this dream reflected a literal history of a former relationship with Vic. It soon became clear that the dream was strictly symbolic for two reasons. First, I have no "holes" in my memory in other areas of my life. Second, I was sure old high school friends who knew about the series would have commented about such an obvious connection.

Symbolically, then, this dream seems to reflect the danger in *romanticizing* the writing process and the presentation of the research in the book. It is true that writing a book demands a passion and commitment similar to that engendered by a romantic relationship. However, it *can* be experienced without the absorption of the romantic archetype. Indeed, the *insanity* of the creative process is very similar to the *insanity* of romance. This is both a *good* thing and a *bad* thing. The sublime highly charged state of passion is as motivating and productive as it is blinding and debilitating. Although that kind of emotional roller coaster was my process of choice when playing the role of "Drama Mama," I was no longer served by the adrenalin loss it demanded. In the overall view of my healing, that frenetic state did not serve me.

I realized that Sally and Sarah represented that archetype because they appeared together in the dream yet do not know each other in the awake world. (When two or more unconnected people appear as a unit in a dream I ask what they have in common. That usually produces the "ah ha" sensation.) Each of these dear old friends commit most of their time and energy to the melodrama of their own grade B romances. Though we see each other infrequently, they spend ninety percent of our time together lamenting yet another man who got away or did them wrong. I often tease that I will not have to see a movie or watch T.V. for a week after our visits as all of my needs for drama have been satisfied!

Reflecting upon my emotional attachment to writing was most revealing and valuable, as this dream occurred when I was questioning the process I had chosen to write this book. I worried that being detached from the book on my weeks off devalued and harmed the project. However, the dream says that *if* I have a desperate romantic attachment I *will have to* abandon the project! (*I worry that, if this suggestion is true, the premise of the book will be destroyed. Then I will have to abandon the project I have come to love.*) I suspected that abandonment would result from physical and emotional burnout before the project was complete.

In addition, there is a *shadow* or not-yet-conscious aspect of this dream. I identified it because of the charged value judgments in the dream. (*I was* totally irritated *with them because of their* infantile *romantic perspective.*) I have learned that feeling neutral about an individual or issue means it is not active within me, not a problem for me. Perhaps I have worked through it and am not now in conflict or in denial about this personality or conceptual issue. But the language chosen to write this dream showed my intense disdain for romantic attachments like those Sally and Sarah choose. I clearly needed to see what that reflected.

At the time of this dream I had been writing for a year. The research was coming together, a wonderful editor had appeared, and it became clear that I was *really* writing a book. Other writers and knowledgeable friends had begun talking to me about the next steps of finding agents and publishers. Dealing with this part of the process did not thrill me. In addition, the ideas of promotional tours encased my heart in cold ice.

By examining the romantic responses of my "shadow" friends, Sarah and Sally, I recognized the kind of passion and attachment I would need to continue to slosh through the rest of the process. This allowed me to see value in the kind of intensity aroused by blind romantic reactions. Making this connection released the negative charge about the dream and about Sally and Sarah. Indeed, my own version of their passionate energy has become valuable and tangible as this project has continued.

In addition, my concerns were addressed by three authors in a span of two weeks. Each of them spontaneously shared the enjoyment and satisfaction they were getting *while* promoting their books. Like me, none of them had anticipated this positive response.

The next dream deals with a way in which my family script created limitations for my thinking process. Take note of the shift in attitude and energy as I work the dream. It clearly shows the power that rushes to the surface when the conscious self is able to understand an important dream symbol.

Old, Set Patterns   AUGUST 15, 1993

I'm in Vic's childhood home chatting with him and his mom about the closure of military bases. I report happily that Fort Ord (the base in my area) has been closed.

My long, vibrant, thick hair is set in pin-curls. I'm embarrassed when I remember this and swiftly brush out this luxurious, shiny mass. I'm upset because it hasn't curled correctly, and I'm really glad I have my electric hair curler with me.

Now we're talking about the book which has resulted from the Victor dream series. As we chat excitedly I'm aware that we're zipping down the freeway seemingly without aid of vehicle. It's as if we're floating in unison on this five-lane freeway. I notice that there are few other cars. How lovely to live in a place that supplies such easy travel without the usual resistance.

My dream journal records an unusual response to this piece. "I feel surprisingly lethargic about recording and working on this piece, when normally a Vic dream is very motivating. Regardless, I will work with it."

The first symbol I tackled was *hair* as it was *idiosyncratic* (not true to awake life) and it was charged with emotion. Though hair can represent persona and self-concept, it is often the outgrowth of the intellect and shows thinking processes. Therefore, long, vibrant, luxurious hair could represent thinking differently than I did at the time of this dream when my finely textured hair was cut very short. It could also symbolize expansive, vibrant beliefs and a very different self-concept.

The hair in this dream is not just *hair*. This is television-commercial hair; long, flowing, expansive as Niagara Falls. This is the kind of hair that, when tossed, knocks over lamps and strangles napping cats. This hair could keep a body alive in below zero weather without benefit of clothing. If hair is a symbol for thinking, then this abundant representation is definitely not the kind of thinking recognized as possible within my family system.

The dream says that my different and massive thinking process has been controlled and formed incorrectly by *old-fashioned bobbie pins*. This is the way my mother *set* her hair all the years she lived. It appears that psyche wanted me to recognize that my possibilites were being controlled by my mother's script. I needed to vividly remember how her thinking processes and resultant world view were controlled by difficult circumstances, fear, depression, helplessness, and cultural expectations which severely limited women.

My journal records this: "In Vic's place, I'm releasing old *S E T* ways of thinking that are not right and need today's *tools* (curling iron) to re-form! My face tingles as I write this. I begin to feel energy and excitement flowing. It's as if the part of me that was crimped and pinned has just now been released. The lethargy/depression with which I began working on this dream has transformed into awe and joy. It's important to note that the *S E T* patterns are released *after* recognition that the former *defense system* (army base) no longer exists!"

Writing that statement brought the thrilling realization that, indeed, a majority of my former defensive coping mechanisms had dramatically receded, allowing me to feel safe even when vulnerable or exposed. I recalled the hated dream from two years before (*Crooked Covered-Up Vic in Kitchen*, Chapter Thirteen), in which my needs to defend myself (symbolized by the clunky bracelet which *armed* me) caused others to reject me. It's always reinforcing to see such progress reflected in dreams.

Shortly before this dream I had begun rewriting sections of this book dealing with family history. Advisors had urged me to tell more of my own story than I originally was prepared to do. My discomfort with this was obvious and I soon had the dream in which my mother had hysterics about the book. I could identify strong inner reticence as I wrote about my family's dysfunction. Disclosing intimate information was as embarrassing as opening a filthy closet in front of strangers. That embarrassment is reflected in the dream (dream ego is embarrassed when she remembers that her hair is in pin-curls).

When I move with Vic and his mother's energy, *then* I am able to discuss the book and fly down the *freeway* (move in the collective) without *resistance*.

What about my strange initial reaction to this dream? I pay close attention to feelings of lethargy and unwillingness to work a dream. I have learned that these examples of resistance always surface when an old script has taken hold and does not wish to relinquish its *set* ways. From that day to this, writing and talking about family issues in public has become much less difficult. As is usual with this series, the directions I receive from the dreams break additional strands of the strangling web, for voicing personal truth is the antithesis of strangulation and repression.

The following dream is one of my all-time favorites. It provided a great sense of relief during a transitional time which occurred unexpectedly during the writing of this book. First, the dream. The explanation follows.

Sheriff Biento!   FEBRUARY 18, 1994

We're in a former ghost town from the gold rush days. The town has been revived and now hosts a small but diverse group of interesting souls. There is a sense of reunion about this trip, as my traveling companion and I are planning to meet other "old" friends.

As we unpack in the La Fonda Hotel, we're told that Victor Biento is the historian/sheriff here. I'm thrilled because I'll surely be able to meet him and tell him about the book.

We meet. Vic's daughter is present. Amidst a lot of activity in what might be a General Store, Vic and I make love standing up. I'm surprised by the swiftness of his orgasm, for which he apologizes and explains. I understand and accept.

I had been feeling uncomfortable, almost anxious at bedtime. I was assailed by a slightly queasy feeling of *Stop the World! I Want to Get Off.* I hoped a dream would clarify my unease. My wishes were answered in spades. I had no resistance to working this charming piece.

Always interested in the environment of a dream—as it sets the stage, so to speak—I examined the meaning of a *ghost town*. I realized that to be in a *revived ghost town* was to be in state of consciousness (or part of my self) which was formerly abandoned. This was once a place of great value *(gold town)* which has been reborn *(revived)*. My dream journal reports this emotional connection: "This is a perfect description of how I feel now about my life in general. I truly feel that I'm digging into precious elements of my eternal *(gold)*

Self, long abandoned." By that I meant a feeling of possibility and potency beyond my personality, beyond my ego, beyond my past.

The *interesting souls* were manifesting both in my awake life as actual people and internally in my burgeoning sense of self. This coming together of energies felt like a reunion, an integration of formerly abandoned parts of myself.

I adore the *La Fonda Hotel* in Santa Fe, New Mexico—my favorite little city. Thus, I was in a wonderful place in my psyche, a truly adored state of being. When in that place I meet the *historian/sheriff*, that which knows the past (historian) and keeps it safe (sheriff). It's as if the extricator of the eagle has resided within me forever, as if *he* is an historical, internal guardian. That he is the *keeper of the law* in this special place brings a sense of light-handed and humorous control.

Victor's daughter is the feminine product of or that which has resulted from, been born from the Victor energy. She was first imaged in a dream in 1988. The daughter symbolizes that which has resulted from the intrapsychic connection with Victor, my new career, and healed life. In addition, I feel her presence in a fresh, new, intuitive softness and acceptance which is now guiding my life, both personal and professional.

To make love in a public place seems like the shameless coming together *in the collective* with that so long sought. Without such a coming together this work would not be carried into the collective arena. *Making love standing up* is a common occurrence in my dream world, and always connects me with men who are the movers and shakers in the world, powerful and successful animus figures. It's as if this visualizes blending with the masculine on the run, ready to move, not lolly-gagging around.

The final realization of the dream caused gales of laughter: To be surprised by the swiftness of Vic's orgasm is to be amazed at how soon this energy has *come!* Suddenly, Victor, the energy I had sought for twenty years (the reunion dreams) and been guided by for an additional twelve years, was no longer simply a possibility for the future—he was a reality in the moment. I had told someone the day before the dream that I was running as fast as I could to keep up with the naturally unfolding events of my life. In the two preceding weeks I had begun working with a professional editor for this book and another. With her encouragement I switched writing systems mid-project by suddenly investing in a computer and printer. I had agreed to do two lectures within a month and had received outstanding reviews about Dream Dance tapes in psychological journals. I was amazed at how swiftly all of these unexpected events had *come* about. A part of me wanted to slow down, but I must *understand and accept the swiftness of the coming,* nonetheless. This reassuring awareness settled into my body as a great sense of rightness and peace in the entire process of expansion.

Though all of the professional developments in my life felt right, this amount of decision-making and action was a bit unusual for my placid life. However, after the reassurance from Vic and a great deal of laughter at the metaphors, all concern dissolved. The world did not have to stop, after all. I simply needed to continue to trust the explicit unfolding of my process guided by "Vic" and other dream images.

INNER EXPLORATION

Process Dreams

- Look at dreams about driving cars, riding bikes, sailing boats, climbing mountains, lazing around, and any other metaphors for activity or inactivity as representing the way we do what we do. For instance, a common dream motif is that of driving an out-of-control car. The specificity of the *out-of-control-ness* is significant. Sliding backwards without brakes suggests one kind of problem; having insufficient power to get to the top of hill suggests something else.

- With a vehicle dream consider who is driving. To *be driven* is a very different metaphor from being in control, in the driver's seat.

- Imagine what it is to *be driven by* a certain kind of individual, and see if that characteristic is active within you. For example, being the passenger in an endangered car driven by one's partner could relate to actual relationship issues or could suggest a psychospiritual attribute which the partner represents.

- For example, a man who associates depression, lethargy, and withdrawal with his father might be warned of being overtaken by ("driven by") those tendencies when he dreams of being a passenger in his own car. When his *father* is in control, the car can't get over the hill. This might reflect the takeover of an attitude that is rendering the dreamer impotent in his awake life.

- Bicycle dreams may reflect a balanced way in which the rider is moving under his own power. Riding a wild stallion presents very different possibilities, though one needs to be balanced in this case as well.

CHAPTER NINETEEN

Imperfection

It takes a lot of nerve to believe that we can or should be able to outwit natural laws, but *perfectionism* requires just that. As a strategy evolved to ensure love and approval, [perfectionism] is rooted deep in the fears and longings of childhood, making it an emotional need, not an intellectual choice.

Joan Borysenko, Ph.D.,
Guilt is the Teacher, Love is the Lesson

This chapter contains two Victor dreams that led me to examine the mechanism of *perfectionism* and identify it as a powerful strand of the web binding the eagle. These dreams allowed me to see that my belief in the existence and necessity of perfect behavior, accomplishment, people, situations, and places immobilized me in many ways. To accommodate growth, I had to be willing to relinquish all beliefs that fostered futile attempts to create a perfect world. I then was able to accept myself, other people, and life, and to function very differently, internally and externally. Once I had stilled the badgering internal voices which stifle, repress, and attempt to reform and conform, I was able to hear the loving, transformational voices which truly heal.

The following dream occurred one week before my first presentation at an international conference on the study of dreams. I had awakened at 4:00 A.M. with an anxiety attack stemming from exposure there. The primary feeling was wanting to return to more security. *Perhaps I could return to public school teaching*, I thought. Happily, I was able to recognize that thought as a primitive contraction/protection impulse. Always willing to use the dream as a source of mental and emotional restructuring, I asked for a dream to deal with the fear. Up popped good old Vic.

The Missed Basket   JUNE 15, 1992

On a college campus I'm delighted to see Vic Biento and immediately yell, "Vic Biento! Get over here!" He charges to me, laughing. He seems much taller than I remember him to be. We talk about the final basketball game of our senior year in which Vic threw the last ball of the game for the winning point as the buzzer sounded. He missed. I'm feeling sorry for him but he seems unconcerned and speaks philosophically about imperfection.

The anxiety I felt before the dream was replaced by Vic's light, cavalier mood. As I pondered the dream I realized that, as far as I could recall, Vic did not play basketball in high school. But I did. I played poorly amidst great ridicule. I recalled a repeating dream series about playing basketball in which I always felt an intense sense of inadequacy and anxiety at the free-throw line. So psyche had chosen a *perfect* image to reconnect me to my trauma in hitting the mark in a public arena. Vic, my rescuer, heals those old deeply imbedded and nearly forgotten wounds by showing the unimportance of making a mistake. He models an ease with imperfection which I desperately needed to continue the eagle's flight.

Much relieved, I returned to sleep to dream the following:

Message Conveyed   JUNE 15, 1992 (CONTINUED)

Now Vic and I are sitting on what seems like a stationary conveyor belt. I'm feeling like a very needy little girl. I whine that I want to be with him always. He patiently explains that this is impossible since he's an ideal. I'm trying to manipulate him with my sadness but he won't budge from his position.

I detest the portrait painted by this dream. It exposes the immature, demanding, and manipulative self, seeking idealistic perfection. The fear that leads to a desire to return to old ways (*teaching school*), attempts to renew a sense of security. In truth, that desire sought by the *whiny one*, ensnares the eagle in her web, destroying the expanding self.

The philosophical implication of this dream is broad and vitally important for my overall physical recovery and my soul. At the strictly mundane level it was equally valuable on the day of my presentation at the conference. The friend who picked me up noticed that the hem in my dress had ripped in the back.

As I charged into the house to throw on something else, my friend's car began smoking and gushing oil. This forced us to take mine, ungassed, unprepared. At the conference we experienced logistic and personnel problems which tried everyone's patience. However, with each disturbance I was able to rebound with aplomb. Being relaxed and *philosophical* about imperfection allowed me to have a wonderful time. I was able to deal easily with all the *missed baskets.*

Minimizing the importance of this dream to the activities of one single day might be called "dream abuse." I had been wrangling consciously with perfectionism for many years. However, *Missed Basket* was the first of my dreams to deal with this important dynamic. Six months later another dream surfaced which dealt with this issue. It highlighted concerns that a developing nurturing mother figure might relapse into insanity. This informed me that I was making progress but was still unsure of my recovery.

Mother, Vic, and the Animals   JANUARY 19, 1993)

I have been working and return home to find the windows washed, the house sparkling clean and dinner on the stove. Because mother is healthy and vigorous she has been enjoying helping me. I'm grateful but worried that she will relapse, forcing me to once again care for a crazy person. I breathe a sigh of relief that, at the moment, all looks very well indeed.

Now I can do my job of tending the animals outside. Some are in cages, others roam around free, but all need care. Vic Biento comes through the carport to help. He's wearing extremely expensive, stunning black leather pants. They get splattered with water as we work. This distresses me enormously. Vic says not to worry, as these pants were made for

this kind of use. As he says this I realize that leather is the
natural protection for such a job and that spilling is inevitable.

The image of the healthy but untrustworthy mother called forth a potent childhood fear. This is always a sure way for psyche to get my attention. As I studied the mother image I saw the cause and effect statement: *when* my internal, nurturing parent is functional and trustworthy, *then* I can help Vic tend to the instinctive, natural, animal energy. In this dream the energy I'm helping (Vic) is prepared for imperfection, for the splashes and stains of life. As dream ego watches the important force she is to help, she realizes that stains are inevitable.

I was intrigued by the animals in this dream. My dreams had never before associated Victor with that kind of energy. I needed to understand what *tending to animal energy* meant. Is it to care for that which is natural, genuine, without self-conscious persona? Is it to be freed from the human process of comparison? (I doubt that animals sit around comparing the shine, length, and color of their coats!) Is it to deal with that which lives without worrying about the past or the future (for animals seem to be always in the moment)? Is it to value instinctive knowing and be rid of the incessant intellectual weighing of this and wondering about that? As far as I can tell the deer I pass on my early morning walks are not bothered by conflict or rationalizations. They know what is potentially harmful and flee from it immediately. Otherwise, they are peacefully aware.

In *The Way of the Dream* written by Frasier Boa, Marie-Louise von Franz suggests that animal nature is (or leads us to) creative productivity. I see this as living a creative life in general, one that is consistently new and different because it is created afresh as the natural, genuine self emerges. This is very different from the life I led before the Eagle Dream urged me into growth. At that time I was usually unconsciously following a script written by my family and culture. Even acts of rebellion did not spring from freedom, for my rebel was simply pushing against a previous script rather than choosing freely.

On the other hand, to live naturally and creatively is to embrace and work with the flow of the Universe. It is to create oneself anew through the consistent inner work of the dream, journal writing, meditating, and, in my case, recovery from addiction and chronic illness. I realized that this kind of creativity has been tended since the Eagle Dream shocked me into consciousness. I was grateful to see that dream ego is working with Vic in the piece. After searching for him for several decades, the connection and cooperation seen in this piece brought a great sense of strength on days when progress was hard to see.

Surely a consistent goal of the Victor Biento series, of all dream work, is to discover, uncover, recover, and activate the natural self, the authentic person we were born to be. Recovering that natural self requires as much awareness of who we are *not* as of who we *authentically are*. This is the value of understanding family and cultural scripting and conditioning. Separating ourselves from our unconscious dictates and modeling is imperative for this natural self to evolve. Clarissa Pinkola Estés says it this way in *Women Who Run With the Wolves:* "When women reassert their relationship with the wildish nature, they are gifted with a permanent and internal watcher, a knower, a visionary, an oracle, an inspiratrice, an intuitive, a maker, a creator, an inventor, and a listener who guide, suggest and urge vibrant life in the inner and outer worlds." It is that kind of vibrant living demanded by the Eagle Dream. Without question, this inner energy known as Victor Biento has been a primary force in escaping the internal elements that try to squelch that vibrancy.

The next dream brings up some changes necessary for continuing this part of my healing process.

Blonde Hair for Victor   MARCH 3, 1994

It's morning. I awake with Vic Biento beside me in bed. I see that we have placed tapered candles on the windowsill above the bed. One has fallen over and put itself out without starting a fire. Alice is in the room, criticizing me because the multicolored sheets have juice and ink spilled on them. Despite finger-pointing Alice, I realize that the spills do not destroy the beauty of the sheets. They are simply incorporated into the design.

Now I turn my attention to Vic. We're comfortable and happy together. He is wondering about his hair color. Should he bleach it blonde? As I run my fingers through his hair, I see that different sections are different colors as if dyed several times with different shades. As we discuss options, I tell him that one old section needs to have the chemicals removed as it is tinged green. I like the natural salt and pepper of the short hairs around his neck area but he really wants it lightened up. Not to worry, I say. I have a variety of colors as well as the solution to remove the unwanted chemicals. We can easily do whatever he wants.

When I am intimately connected to *(in bed with)* this important energy named Victor I can realize that spills and stains *(imperfections)* are just part of the whole. Within this context this Victor energy wants to further *lighten up* his thinking processes and presentation of self *(hair* as persona). This lightening process has been through several different stages already *(different colors)*. One old process *(unwanted chemicals)* has gone bad and must be removed altogether. Dream ego is prepared to do whatever Victor calls for; she already has all that is needed to change, to lighten up.

Before this dream I never realized how very heavy and dark perfection-ism feels. I recalled the bad old days of compulsive tidiness when I would read-ily jump out of my chair to straighten a candle, destroying an intensely important conversation. As I recalled the compelling inner energy employed to make things, myself, and others perfect, I relived the darkness which results from needing to see everything "just so." This is not a place of acceptance, comfort or options. That drive to force, pound, manipulate and mold the world into some image of perfection is dense, opaque, unmoveable. It hurts and is hurtful to others. These realizations brought a deep sadness to the sur-face. Facing this part of my shadow and the pain it had caused in the past allowed me to feel extremely grateful for the progress made in *lightening* my perceptions and thinking processes.

At the time of this dream I'd experienced eleven years of recovery and several different stages—or in this dream's language, several different *hair col-ors*—in lightening up. Early in my physical healing I had realized a connec-tion between chronic fatigue and chronic perfectionism. It's difficult to really rest, totally let down, in a world which constantly creates dust in the house, wind to fell the leaves in the garden, and humans who do not follow the script I have written. My perfectionistic mind was never at peace because someone, some problem, or some part of myself always obsessively needed attention. Releasing those compulsive/obsessive dictates has been imperative for the recovery of my endocrine and immune systems.

Learning to recognize that spilled candles and ink stains are part of the entire pattern of human life has significantly altered my perception and accep-tance of the world. Since the world I see "out there" is truly a reflection of the one between my ears, this acceptance had to start with myself. When I forget this I encounter the whiny little girl on the conveyor belt demanding constant connection to an idealized life. Dealing with her in a gentle loving way always produces a shift wherein I see that imperfections of all kinds simply blend into the whole of life.

INNER EXPLORATION
Hair in Dreams

- If a dream spotlights hair in some way, consider whether you are dealing with issues of *persona* (roles we play in the world, ways that we present ourselves to others) or with beliefs and ideas.

- What characteristics do you attribute to blondes, brunettes, red-heads, gray and white heads, bald heads, and long hair on men and short hair on women? These judgments probably will be reflected in your dreams.

- Pay attention if your dream hair is different from your awake style, color, texture. What do the changes suggest to you in terms of self-image? In terms of beliefs? Would it be a good idea for these changes to be embraced?

- If your dream hair looks as it did at another time in your life, consider in what ways you might be thinking, feeling, or acting as you did then.

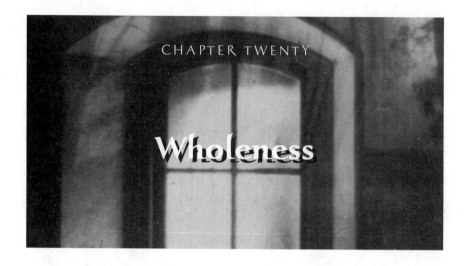

CHAPTER TWENTY

Wholeness

The Self can be defined as an inner guiding factor that is different from the conscious personality and that can be grasped only through the investigation of one's own dreams. These show it to be the regulating center that brings about a constant extension and maturing of the personality. But this larger, more nearly total aspect of the psyche appears first as merely an inborn possibility. It may emerge very slightly, or it may develop relatively completely during one's lifetime. How far it develops depends on whether or not the ego is willing to listen to the messages of the Self.

Marie-Louise von Franz, in *Man and His Symbols* by C.G. Jung

If self embraces both consciousness and unconsciousness, then those moments when we transform or transmute an event into an experience, when we are connected, inner to outer, are moments when we experience Self.

Peter O'Connor, *Dreams and the Search for Meaning*

I began researching the Victor Biento series in hopes of discovering and understanding the patterns created by more than a hundred dreams with repeating elements, scattered over more than thirty-five years. Hoping that seeing all the pieces together would create something useful, I began with curiosity, a great deal of confusion, and just enough willingness. Obviously, I worked from the presumption that dreams are developmentally valuable and potentially healing. Except for the belief that the study would be revealing, I had no notion of what had been, or wanted to be created as I examined my sleep art.

At the beginning I knew that the imprisoned Eagle had catapulted me into an intense awareness of the dream process. That led to the discovery that I was working with two distinct dream strands—the Reunion Series and the Victor Biento dreams. What their blending would reveal I did not know at the initiation of this work.

As I review the entire process of writing this book I am impressed by how emotionally tumultuous inner work can be. I still feel the vivid horror and grief evoked by seeing the eagle caught in the web. How stunned I was to discover that the repetitive dream character, Victor, was an actual person from my adolescent past. Realizing that dying dream Victor metaphorically represented my physical condition electrified me for several days. Recognizing that the work with Victor continuously returned me to unresolved past issues always surprised me. Identifying that the Victor series addressed all the major inner and outer processes of my life intrigued me. I was enormously thrilled when enough pieces came together to identify Victor as the potential *extractor of the eagle*. Seeing that what I had been seeking had *provided the way* for me to reach it continues to delight me. And the power of Victor's unconditional acceptance of me—oozing face and all—brings comfort even today. Each profound "ah ha," combined with dozens of others less dramatic, connected me more and more deeply to an inner force determined to help me live fully. Most profound of all, for more than thirty-five years I have been compelled to follow a quietly rebellious force which has consistently encouraged me to consciously create and live an authentic life of personal integrity.

As the dream patterns drew into focus I saw the tapes, the repetitious familial and cultural beliefs and behaviors which had created and maintained *dis-ease* at every level of my being. Equally significant were the gentle, loving, often humorous dream suggestions that dissolved the sticky web of destruction and repression that had imprisoned me for so many years. In short, after enough pieces came together, I clearly saw the shattered parts of my self becoming integrated into the total restructuring of my life. Those tasks accomplished, I am joyfully left with a healed body/mind which feels deeply reunited with my soul. In short, I have a sense of unity and wholeness never experienced *before* the work on this book was begun.

Notice the phrase, *before the work on this book was begun.* Obviously individual dreams impacted my waking self, bringing attitudinal and behavioral changes throughout the years. But I never experienced the overall majesty, the sense of a definite plan, and the blueprint for healing and wholeness that appeared *until* all the separate pieces were stitched together. Only then, because of this work, did I truly *experience* the theory presented by Carl Jung that there is, indeed, an inner force which he called the Self which is repeatedly sketching the form of who we are to become. However, to see it clearly, this guiding power needs our *conscious* involvement. Finally, now that the manuscript is nearly complete, I feel as if my partnership with psyche has begun to create a full and whole illustration.

The following two dreams beautifully exemplify that feeling of completion.

Four-Play with Vic   NOVEMBER 22, 1992

I feel young—high school age—but I look as I do now. There is a party going on in my present house. Mother is happily

helping in another room. Vic leads me to the bedroom, which
is cluttered with knick-knacks.

Vic and I lie on the bed to play around. He says that he
will forever love anyone who traces four patterns on his back.
I am happy to oblige. I hope and suspect this is a sexual ploy.

*I enjoy **his responsiveness** as I trace **four** very creative*
***patterns that flow cleverly one into the other.** I'm con-*
cerned about and focused on the segues *between each pat-*
*tern. **It feels imperative that I connect each pattern in***
***a very specific way.** I become so absorbed in this process of*
accurately moving from one pattern to another that I forget
about Vic.

After recording the dream I was first drawn to understanding the significance of the *four* patterns. Since I have no personal association with the number four, I turned to Jungian sources for suggestions. This, from Max Zeller's
The Dream: The Vision of the Night:

> Four is the number of totality, of wholeness. The *four* directions of
> the compass allow complete orientation in space. We talk about *four*
> walls. *Four* divides the hour into quarters, the year into *four* seasons.
> We talk about the *four* phases of life. The Hindus have *four* castes.
> The ancient philosophers talked about the *four* elements. Jung's *four*
> psychological functions are such a complete map for an orientation
> in the realm of consciousness. The *number four* appears frequently in
> dreams. Whenever that happens the question of *wholeness* is at stake.

With that understanding of *four-ness* I turned my attention to the metaphors from the dream. Though I am mature, I feel young as I celebrate *(party)*
in the presence of a healed nurturing force *(mother)*. I'm led to the place of
intimacy, rejuvenation, and dreaming, *(bedroom)*, surrounded by the past *(knick-
knacks)*. The single most tenacious and transformative force in my psyche gives

me the task of creating wholeness *(four patterns)*. My challenge is to *integrate disparate parts into a whole.*

I liked the blending of the young me with the present me. This felt like the girl, the potential from the past, had been integrated with the adult of today.

As I worked with this dream Vic expanded beyond his former roles to represent the entire force of psyche. Seen that way, accepting the invitation of *psyche* to create wholeness, to willfully engage in the process of individuation, generates an excitement, involvement, presence, and creativity similar to sexual activity. In return, this participation creates a *responsiveness* from psyche which I do truly love. Most frequently I experience that as a universal interplay felt in synchronicities. I am truly *turned on* by the synchronistic sense of give and take, action and reaction, and of the partnership between the inner and outer self and the world beyond self.

Most of dream ego's energy and attention are spent on the connections between the four patterns I am tracing on Victor's back. At the time of this dream, I was diligently occupied with that type of task demanded by the work on this book. The biggest challenge was identifying the segues, the interweaving between the dreams from both dream series. However, I'm sure this dream addresses a much greater and more universal human task, perhaps connecting the physical, emotional, intellectual, and spiritual stratas of the human experience so that each is blended with the others. My striving for a balanced life has necessitated consciously connecting these four aspects gracefully and beautifully. This is a daily challenge. I am sure there is more beyond that which I cannot yet see or articulate.

I was struck by the similarity of *segues* and *merging* when I read this from *Our Dreaming Mind* by Robert Van de Castle: "The Self expresses the unity of the personality as a whole and is based upon a *merging* of the many levels of the unconscious and conscious mind." The merging of the conscious and unconscious minds occurs every time we have an *ah ha* experience. Undoubt-edly, awareness occurs each time a bridge is built from the underground of the dream to the surface of awake life. In addition, I believe that my present sense of unity and wholeness, which was not *experienced* before working with the dream material for this book, is what results from seeing the *merging of the unconscious and conscious mind.*

There can be no doubt by this time that the Victor series has helped to identify and merge many parts of my self. The resultant integration creates an overall sense of balance and peace.

Following is the only dream thus far containing both Victor and the Eagle. It may be that it clearly expresses the purpose of this entire work.

Repairing the Hole   APRIL 4, 1994

I'm sitting on a patio with friends. We see a gigantic eagle hunkered down beside us. I approach it in awe, fearing that it will surely fly away when I get too close. But no, it simply eyes me as I walk towards it.

Now I can study it closely. I see a definite hole in its right wing. We must take it to Victor Biento. He has two colors and types of healing sticks to make a splint for the bird. It will be able to fly if tended to in this way.

I doubt it can ever grow itself over this hole as one repairs a broken bone and eventually discards the cast. I think these healing sticks will always be needed if this magnificent, grounded creature is to soar again.

I can see the eagle's eyes following me as I approach to help it. The hole in the wing is not a tear, like a wound. Instead it is a perfect circle, a genetic inborn defect, not the result of trauma.

> *My friends and I take the bird to Victor to get the heal-*
> *ing sticks. I see that both he and I are needed to reweave this*
> *hole. We will use both colors and types of sticks, the green as*
> *the warp and the blue as the weft. That will be sufficient.*
> *The bird can fly strong and true with this repair.*

Though the eagle is out of the web, she is unable to soar until Vic and I *work together* to mend her, to *repair the hole, the wholeness*. I take this, once again, to mean that the self which makes choices, represented by dream ego, and Victor, the inner psychic energy, *must* join forces to achieve freedom. In a broader context, we must commit our conscious energy to accomplish the goals of psyche before our spirits can fly.

How different this piece would have been had the hole been from a bullet or a fight with another creature. This hole is a definite, inborn, genetic, perfect circle which must be patched by both Victor and dream ego. I see this as the *perfect* symbol for the *imperfection* of the human experience. The inborn defect can be repaired only by a commitment to interweave the conscious and the unconscious. Marie-Louise von Franz says it this way: "Ego has not been produced by nature to follow its own arbitrary impulses to an unlimited extent, but to help to make real the totality—the whole psyche."

The interwoven sticks of consciousness can never be removed. In the dream there was a sense of *rightness* about that process, about the weaving of the sticks, and about their permanence. As I view Victor tending to the eagle, I recognize how that inner psychic force has indeed performed the job of mending the holes in my psyche.

Knowing that there is nothing random in a dream, I reflected on the hole in the *right* wing and recalled the following quote by von Franz in *Man and His Symbols*: "...the right side [is] the side where things become conscious."

As Vic and I have worked together for more than half of my lifetime, virtually every aspect of my being has been altered dramatically. The severely wounded and imprisoned self has been extricated, one nearly invisible but exceedingly powerful strand at a time. The woman with a disintegrating body controlled by a pessimistic, terrified, furious mind has transformed into a person of faith, joy, and health. The former individual, always swift to attack, has become undefended yet feels profoundly safe. The one who harmed others and herself is, hopefully, not only harmless but primarily helpful. After sixteen years of steady work a shattered, disintegrated soul and body has reunited with the authentic, conscious self.

I started this journey with the hope of discovering *who* Victor Biento was in my psyche. Many different theories could be offered, but when all is said and done we can only marvel at the mystery of our dreaming self. We can never define or label, and thus *be sure*. But I am now at peace with the recognition of the majesty of a perpetually healing inner force helping us all to manifest our wholeness. The imposition of that force through the Eagle Dream and my willingness to follow it has *finally* enabled Dream Eagle to soar.

Epilogue

After the completion of this manuscript my connection to dream Victor began to change. The Reunion Series continued by showing dream ego participating in the planning and execution of the reunion activities. That accomplished, the Victor Series took an interesting turn. Victor and dream ego began to live together. At first others were present, as in a group house. Then Victor was presented as the builder of the yet uncompleted home in which he and I were to live. Finally, in the last dream to date, Victor and I are living together in the same house. The dream reads as follows:

The Beautiful, Unexpected Gift!   AUGUST 11, 1996

Victor Biento's sister introduces him to me while he is relaxing in a chair. I am very excited and tell him about the thirty-six year dream series.

Now Victor and I are living together. Since I've moved in with him life has become very exciting. A great deal happens everyday. There is lots of humor, activity and many fascinating people. I love this new life though I am no longer in control of it.

In a wonderful shop Victor and I examine some beautiful Native American inlaid rings. When we arrive home I'm surprised to find several large, beautiful bracelets created by

the same Native American artist. It seems that Victor saw
what I liked and bought me something even better!

Surely that last sentence sums up this entire dream relationship. It appears that dream Victor has always been leading me beyond who I am and what I'm doing to create an inner life and identity that is far more pleasing to me than my ego would have selected on its own. Indeed, this dream relationship has constructed a foundation from which springs potential new life.

The loom of life is strung with many threads. Genetics and gender, historic time, culture and family, personal will and intrinsic talent, fate, the gods and daimons all provide the warp threads upon which psyche can weave her patterns. Spider Woman comes in the dark to add weft to the warp. Dream by dream the strands blend to create a pattern of wholeness.

And so, for the moment, this dream weaving is complete.

Glossary

active imagination: a process of actively working with the unconscious to allow spontaneous images, feelings, and awarenesses to occur. This is experienced as a dialogue between the conscious "awake" self and the unconscious self.

archetype: a representation which is thought to influence behaviors and experiences common to all humans regardless of race, culture, or historical time. Just as animals are driven by biological instincts, so people are motivated by psychological "instincts" or archetypes.

awake ego: the person you know yourself to be while conscious, while in the awake world.

dream ego: the character or person the dreamer feels her/himself to be in the dream. This dream element is most like the awake self and usually reflects the same values, opinions, and feelings.

denial: a type of defense utilized to avoid feeling painful circumstances or to disregard parts of the self.

individuation: the process of development or evolution during which the parts of the self are united, creating a sense of wholeness. This is a process of discovering and living the authentic self rather than the self adapted to the demands of others.

integration: the act or process of bringing together separate parts of the self. This results in a sense of congruence and authenticity.

peak experience: an experience beyond the usual which vitalizes, infuses with hope, and allows a broader view of reality than previously known.

persona: the masks we wear or roles we play in order to feel accepted and safe. This is the self presented to the world.

psyche: understood as a container which holds all of our conscious and unconscious processes. This is the place from which dreams and all creative work emanate.

repression: a defense during which change or alteration to the family or cultural script is relinquished to the unconscious rather than acted out.

recovery: the process of healing from addiction or mental or physical illness or malaise.

REM: the sleep state in which dreaming occurs and during which the eyes of the dreamer move rapidly, thus, *rapid eye movement.*

script: as in a theatrical production, that which contains the unconscious roles that we play and the identities that we assume as demanded by our family (family script) or culture (cultural script).

shadow: aspects of the self which are unconscious or unlived.

soul: the deep, authentic, animating part of a living organism.

transpersonal: beyond the usual, the mundane. Experiences and knowing which create a sense of connection to a universal source or power beyond the ego.

totem: a symbol, usually an animal, which is thought to represent and guide the self.

Bibliography

Andrews, Ted. *Animal-Speak*. St. Paul, MI: Llewellyn Publications, 1995.

Baldwin, Christina. *Life's Companion*. New York: Bantam Books, 1991.

Beattie, Melody. *A Codependent's Guide to the Twelve Steps*. New York: Simon & Schuster, 1993.

Berne, Eric. *A Layman's Guide to Psychiatry and Psychoanalysis*. New York: Simon & Schuster, 1968.

_____. *Transactional Analysis in Psychotherapy*. Edison, NJ: Castle Books, 1961.

Bly, Robert. *The Little Book on the Human Shadow*. San Francisco: Harper Row Publishers, 1988.

Boa, Frasier. *The Way of the Dream*. Toronto: Windrose Films United, 1994.

Borysenko, Joan. *Fire in the Soul*. New York: Warner Books, 1993.

_____. *Guilt is the Teacher, Love is the Lesson*. New York: Warner Books, 1989.

_____. *Minding the Body; Mending the Mind*. Reading, MA: Addison-Wesley Publishing Company, Inc., 1987.

Bradshaw, John. *Healing the Shame that Binds You*. Deerfield Beach, FL: Health Communications, Inc., 1988.

_____. *Homecoming*. New York: Bantam Books, 1990.

Cameron, Julia and Mark Bryan. *The Artist's Way*. New York: (A Jeremy P. Tarcher/Putnam Book) G.P. Putnam's Sons, 1992.

Cameron, Julia. *The Vein of Gold*. New York: (A Jeremy P. Tarcher/Putnam Book) G.P. Putnam's Sons, 1996.

Campbell, Joseph. *The Hero with a Thousand Faces*. Princeton: Princeton University Press, 1948.

Carlson, Richard and Benjamin Shield, eds. *Healers on Healing*. Los Angeles: J.P. Tarcher, 1989.

Chopra, Deepak. *Quantum Healing*. New York: Bantam Books, 1989.

_____. *Unconditional Life*. New York: Bantam Books, 1991.

Clift, Jean Dalby and Wallace B. Clift. *Symbols of Transformation in Dreams*. New York: Crossroad Publishing Co., 1993.

_____. *The Hero Journey in Dreams*. New York: Crossroad Publishing Co., 1991.

Coelho, Paulo. *The Alchemist*. Translated by Alan R. Clarke. New York: Harper Collins Publishers, 1993.

Corriere, Richard and Joseph Hart. *The Dream Makers*. New York: Funk and Wagnalls, 1977.

Delaney, Gayle. *Breakthrough Dreaming*. New York: Bantam Books, 1991.

_____. *Living your Dreams*. San Francisco: Harper and Row, 1979.

Dossey, Larry. *Meaning and Medicine*. New York: Bantam Books, 1991.

_____. *Healing Words*. San Francisco: Harper San Francisco, 1993.

Estés, Clarissa Pinkola. *Women Who Run With the Wolves*. New York: Ballantine Books, 1992, 1995.

Faraday, Ann. *The Dream Game*. New York: Harper and Row, 1974.

_____. *Dream Power*. New York: Berkeley Books, 1972.

_____. *Creative Dreaming*. New York: Ballantine Books, 1974.

_____. *Pathway to Ecstasy*. New York: Prentice Hall, 1979.

Gendlin, Eugene T. *Let your Body Interpret your Dreams*. Wilmette, IL: Chiron Publications, 1986.

Hall, Calvin. *The Meaning of Dreams* (rev. ed.). New York: McGraw Hill, 1966.

_____. *Jungian Dream Interpretation*. Toronto: Inner City Books, 1983.

Hannah, Barbara. *Jung*. New York: G.P. Putnam's Sons, 1976.

Harris, Thomas A. *I'm OK, You're OK*. New York: Harper and Row, 1967.

Hillman, James. *A Blue Fire*. New York: Harper and Row, 1989.

_____. *The Soul's Code*. New York: Random House, 1996.

Hull, R.F.C., trans. *Dreams: C.G. Jung*. Princeton: Princeton University Press, 1974.

James, William. *The Varieties of Religious Experience*. Cambridge: Harvard University Press, 1985.

Johnson, Robert. *Inner Work*. San Francisco: Harper and Row, 1986.

Jung, C.G. *The Collected Works*. ed. H. Read, M. Fordham and G. Adler. Princeton: Princeton University Press, 1953–60. London: Routledge. New York: Pantheon Books, 1953–60. New York: Bollingen Foundation, 1961–78.

Jung, C.G. *Man and His Symbols*. Chicago: Ferguson Publishing Company, 1978.

_____. *Memories, Dreams and Reflections*. London: Routledge & Kegan Paul, 1963. New York: Random House, 1965.

Kaplan-Williams, Strephon. *Dreamworking*. San Francisco: Journey Press, 1991.

Keen, Sam. *The Passionate Life: Stages of Loving*. New York: Harper Collins Publishers, 1983.

Keen, Sam and Anne Valley-Fox. *Your Mythic Journey*. New York: G.P. Putnam's Sons, 1989.

Kelser, Kenneth. *The Sun and the Shadow*. Virginia Beach: A.R.E. Press, 1987.

Krippner, Stanley, ed. *Dreamtime and Dreamwork*. Los Angeles: J.P. Tarcher, 1990.

Leonard, George. *The Silent Pulse*. New York: The Penguin Group, 1978, 1986.

Levine, Barbara. *Your Body Believes Every Word You Say*. Boulder Creek, CA: Aslan Publishing, 1991.

Mambert, W.A. and Frank B. Foster. *A Trip into your Unconscious*. Washington D.C.: Acropolis Books Ltd., 1973.

Mahoney, Maria F. *The Meaning in Dreams and Dreaming*. Secaucus, NJ: The Citadel Press, 1966.

Mindell, Arnold. *Working with the Dreaming Body*. Boston: Routledge and Kegan Paul, 1985.

Moore, Thomas. *Care of the Soul*. New York: Harper Collins Publishers, 1992.

Pelletier, Kenneth R. *Mind as Healer; Mind as Slayer.* New York: Dell Publishing, 1977.

Perls, Frederick. *Gestalt Therapy Verbatim.* Lafayette, CA: Real People Press, 1969.

Perls, Frederick, Ralph F. Hefferline, and Paul Goodman. *Gestalt Therapy.* New York: Dell Publishing, 1951.

Progoff, Ira. *At a Journal Workshop.* New York: Dialogue House Library, 1975.

Raheem, Aminah. *Soul Return.* Santa Rosa, CA: Aslan Publishing, 1987, 1991.

Rossi, Ernest. *Dreams and the Growth of Personality.* Elmsford, NY: Pergamon Press, Inc., 1972.

Sanford, John. *Healing and Wholeness.* New Jersey: Paulist Press, 1977.

_____. *Dreams, Gods, Forgotten Language.* New York: Crossroad Publishing, 1984.

Savary, Louis. "Dreams and Spiritual Energy" and "Dreamtime" in *ASD Journal.* Vienna, VA: Association for the Study of Dreams, Vol. 13, Number 1, Spring, 1996.

Scarf, Maggie. *Body, Mind, Behavior.* New York: Dell Publishing Co., Inc., 1977.

Schaef, Anne Wilson. *Beyond Therapy, Beyond Science.* San Francisco: Harper Collins, 1992.

Sinetar, Marsha. *Do What You Love and the Money will Follow.* New York: Paulist Press, 1987.

Siegel, Bernie. *Love, Medicine and Miracles.* New York: Harper and Row, 1986.

Signell, Karen. *Wisdom of the Heart.* New York: Bantam, 1990.

Singer, June. *Seeing Through the Visible World.* New York: Harper Collins Publishers, 1991.

Small, Jacquelyn. *Transformers: The Artists of Self Creation.* New York: Bantam Books, 1992.

Steiner, Claude. *Scripts People Live.* New York: Grove Press, 1974.

Stevens, Anthony. *Private Myths.* Cambridge, MA: Harvard University Press, 1995.

Strutt, Malcolm. *Wholistic Health and Living Yoga.* Boulder Creek, CA: University of the Trees Press, 1976.

Talbot, Michael. *The Holographic Universe.* New York: Harper Perennial, 1991.

Taylor, Jeremy. *Where People Fly and Water Runs Uphill*. New York: Warner Books, 1992.

Tart, Charles T. *Waking Up*. Boston: Shambhala, 1987.

_____, ed. *Altered States of Consciousness*. Garden City: Doubleday/Anchor, 1969.

Ullman, Montigue and Nancy Zimmerman. *Working with Dreams*. New York: Dell Publishing Co., Inc. 1980.

Van de Castle, Robert. *Our Dreaming Mind*. New York: Ballantine Books (Random House, Inc.), 1994.

Vaughan, Frances. *The Inward Arc: Healing in Psychotherapy and Spirituality*. Nevada City, CA: Blue Dolphin Publishing, 1995.

_____. *Shadows of the Sacred*. Wheaton, IL: The Theosophical Publishing House, 1995.

Whitmont, Edward C. and Sylvia Brinton Perera. *Dreams: A Portal to the Source*. London: Routledge Ltd., 1989.

Woodman, Marion. *Addiction to Perfection*. Toronto: Inner City Books, 1982.

Zeller, Max. *The Dream: The Vision of the Night*. Boston: SIGO Press, 1975, 1990.

RELATED BOOKS FROM THE CROSSING PRESS

The Language of Dreams
By Patricia Telesco
Patricia Telesco outlines a creative, interactive approach to understanding the dream symbols of our inner life. Interpretations of more than 800 dream symbols incorporate multi-cultural elements with psychological, religious, folk, and historical meanings.
$16.95 • Paper • 0-89594-836-2

Wishing Well:
Empowering Your Hopes and Dreams
By Patricia Telesco
Blending folklore, magic, and creative visualization, author Patricia Telesco explains how reclaiming the practice of Wishcraft can create our reality exactly as we wish it to be.
$14.95 • Paper • 0-89594-870-2

Pocket Guide to Self Hypnosis
By Adam Burke, Ph. D.
Self-hypnosis and imagery are powerful tools that activate a very creative quality of mind. By following the methods provided, you can begin to make progress on your goals and feel more in control of your life and destiny.
$6.95 • Paper • 0-89594-824-9

Chakras and Their Archetypes:
Uniting Energy Awareness and Spiritual Growth
By Ambika Wauters
Linking classic archetypes to the seven chakras in the human energy system can reveal unconscious ways of behaving. Wauters helps us understand where our energy is blocked, which attitudes or emotional issues are responsible, and how to then transcend our limitiations.
$16.95 • Paper • 0-89594-891-5

Your Body Speaks Your Mind:
How Your thoughts and Emotions Affect Your Health
By Debbie Shapiro
Debbie Shapiro examines the intimate connection between the mind and body revealing insights into how our unresolved thoughts and feelings affect our health and manifest as illness in specific parts of the body.
$14.95 • Paper • 0-89594-893-1

Shamanism as a Spiritual Practice for Daily Life
By Tom Cowan
Drawing on shamanic practices from the world over, including many ancient Western European traditions, Cowan's book addresses the needs of contemporary men and women who yearn for a deeper connection to the natural and spiritual realms.
$16.95 • Paper • 0-89594-838-9

✳

To receive a current catalog from The Crossing Press,
please call toll-free, 800-777-1048.
Visit our Website on the Internet at: www.crossingpress.com